"Ben Lowe has done us all a favor: he has assembled some of the most notable teachers in the world to mentor us on the greatest of coming revolutions. This planet is our great gift from God, but it is also our sobering responsibility to renew for the poor and the coming generations. In these pages you will find the intellectual and practical path forward. This book will develop your strategy and your faith."
Joel C. Hunter, senior pastor, Northland, A Church Distributed, Florida

"Ben Lowe makes a compelling case for the role of colleges and universities in preparing tomorrow's creation care servant leaders. This book is must-reading for those faculty, students and institutional leaders who will be called to teach and model new ways of thinking and living if we are to heal our planet."
Dr. Ed Johnson, president, Au Sable Institute

"Ben writes with a refreshingly youthful and transparent style that is at times penetrating and disturbing, and at other times light and casual. The book is a good read for the Metro—it doesn't require reading in a single setting!"
Paul Corts, president, Council for Christian Colleges and Universities

"A new generation of younger evangelicals is leading the way in showing us how to be mindful of our stewardship for the world in which we live, not as a substitute for biblical faith but as a faithful expression of it. Ben Lowe's book helps us do just that. I recommend it to all Christians everywhere."
Timothy George, dean, Beeson Divinity School, Samford University, and senior editor, *Christianity Today*

"*Green Revolution* is more than a great book. It's a powerfully convincing invitation to join a fresh movement of God. Thanks, Ben Lowe, for your faithful creation witness!"
Jonathan Merritt, faith and culture writer, and national spokesperson, Southern Baptist Environment and Climate Initiative

"Ben Lowe has been an outstanding pioneer of practical caring for creation. His generation is probably the one that most urgently needs to understand and live by the passionate convictions that he has expressed so eloquently in these pages. If they do we may enter a season of hope. If they don't, we are probably, most literally, cooked."
Peter Harris, founder, A Rocha

"I commend this book to all college students and concerned citizens of God's earth. Lowe gets it right! Biblical environmental stewardship is about the transformation of hearts and minds, and about incarnational living on earth. The book's case studies and stories illuminate and provide a useful framework to help Christians relearn what it means to love God, neighbor and creation."
Susan Drake Emmerich, CEO, Emmerich Environmental Consulting, and coproducer, *When Heaven Meets Earth: Faith, Environment and the Chesapeake Bay*

"Ben Lowe writes with a fresh voice about an issue that affects each of us deeply. Pick up this book and join the green revolution today!"
Will Samson, coauthor of *Justice in the Burbs*

Green Revolution

Coming Together to Care for Creation

To Tim,

God give you grace & passion to care for his good creation!

Ben Lowe

Ben Lowe

Foreword by Shane Claiborne

Afterword by J. Matthew Sleeth, M.D.

IVP Books

An imprint of InterVarsity Press
Downers Grove, Illinois

InterVarsity Press
P.O. Box 1400, Downers Grove, IL 60515-1426
World Wide Web: www.ivpress.com
E-mail: email@ivpress.com

InterVarsity Press® is the book-publishing division of InterVarsity Christian Fellowship/USA®, a movement of students and faculty active on campus at hundreds of universities, colleges and schools of nursing in the United States of America, and a member movement of the International Fellowship of Evangelical Students. For information about local and regional activities, write Public Relations Dept., InterVarsity Christian Fellowship/USA, 6400 Schroeder Rd., P.O. Box 7895, Madison, WI 53707-7895, or visit the IVCF website at <www.intervarsity.org>.

Design: Matt Smith
Images: trees: Tsuyoshi Hiratsuka/Sebun Photo/Getty Images
       crowd: Bart Claeys/iStockphoto

ISBN 978-0-8308-3624-6

Printed in the United States of America ∞

Library of Congress Cataloging-in-Publication Data

Lowe, Ben, 1984-
  Green revolution: coming together to care for creation / Ben Lowe.
    p. cm.
  Includes bibliographical references.
  ISBN 978-0-8308-3624-6 (pbk.: alk. paper)
  1. Human ecology—Religious aspects—Christianity. 2. Ecotheology.
  3. Communities—Religious aspects—Christianity. I. Title.
BT695.5.L695 2009
261.8'8—dc22

                                   2008046020

| P | 23 | 22 | 21 | 20 | 19 | 18 | 17 | 16 | 15 | 14 | 13 | 12 | 11 | 10 | 9 | 8 | 7 | 6 | 5 | 4 | 3 |
| Y | 29 | 28 | 27 | 26 | 25 | 24 | 23 | 22 | 21 | 20 | 19 | 18 | 17 | 16 | 15 | 14 | 13 | 12 | 11 | 10 | 09 |

To God,

with awe

for your gifts of this earth and one another,

and for the supreme

sacrifice and triumph of your Son

that saves us

and reconciles all things back to you.

CONTENTS

Foreword

God is moving in the world. Across the globe are signs of a church that is closer to the poor and further from the drums of nationalism and war. We can see an emerging church that looks more like Jesus than the evangelicalism many of us grew up with. But there is still much work to do.

There is so much noise and clutter in the Christian industrial complex. Books line the shelves with advice on how to find our best life, how to live with purpose, how to find God's blessing and the secret to prosperity—all missing the true secret of the gospel, which is that we find our life by giving it away. When we are truly thankful for God's blessings, we cannot help but share them. Too often, we have settled for independence over interdependence and have run after America's dream rather than God's. Our money is branded "In God we trust," but our economy is built on the seven deadly sins. The beautiful thing is that we don't need a guilt trip; we just need an invitation to something better. We need an invitation to dream with God. God's dream is one of a restored creation rather than a groaning one. It is the dream of people beating their swords into farm tools rather than fighting the wars of the nations.

Christian theologians say that some of the most misunderstood verses in the Bible are those dealing with creation. Some Bible versions speak of how the earth will be "destroyed" by fire rather than "refined" by fire—and that makes a big difference. After all, if the world is going to be destroyed, who cares how we live? But things are much different when we believe that the creation is being *refined,* that the ancient ruins are being brought to life again as the prophets proclaim and that our faith is less about us going up and more about God's kingdom coming down . . . on earth as it is in heaven.

That's why I am grateful for Ben Lowe's book. *Green Revolution* is an invitation, not just to believe that another world is possible, but to begin enacting it now.

Jesus did not come just to prepare us to die. Jesus came to teach us how to live. The kingdom of God he proclaimed is not something we are to hope for when we die, but something we are to live out on earth as it is in heaven. In the words of Indian activist Arundhati Roy, "Another world is not only possible, she's on her way. On a quiet day, if I listen very carefully, I can hear her breathing."

Shane Claiborne

Introduction
Why a Revolution?

What the world needs is people who believe so much in another world that they cannot help but begin enacting it now.

Shane Claiborne, *The Irresistible Revolution*

"We need help," Professor Mbutu implored. "Look at all my people living here in poverty. The children, they have no hope for when they grow up. Many cannot afford the basic education, and even that is little good."

Light was fading quickly as we walked back to the hostel after dinner. I could barely make out the huts around me. During daylight I had seen that they were made of mud, homemade bricks and odd pieces of scrap wood. Most had only one room in them; many did not have any power. As we stumbled along the dark, dusty road together, I thought to myself, *Not exactly the living conditions we expect back home in the States.*

It was a warm evening in July 2006. I was there, in the small Tanzanian town of Kigoma, during the summer of my junior year in college, as part of a government-funded research project. The professor was our main local contact and one of the few hydrologists in a country where over half the population lacks access to clean water.

Along the way, Dr. Mbutu shared his dream to make clean water, improved sanitation and good education available to his fellow Tanzanians: "I originally came from this town. Before I was lucky enough to go to the big university, this was my home. In my heart, it is still home. It breaks my heart to see the people suffering. I keep coming back to try to help them. But I am only one man. Can you see that I need your help?"

My mind was struggling to grasp the scale of the need surrounding me, and my words betrayed the despair I felt: "Mwalimu, Teacher, I am only a young person and have little money myself. What can I do?"

His reply came quickly. "You are a Christian, and so am I. We are both

The author collecting data on a local fishing beach in Kigoma, Tanzania. Photo by Jennifer Schmitz.

brothers in Christ. You have many Christians and churches back in America. Get them to help us. We have so little over here—if you work together, it does not take much to make a big difference."

Dr. Mbutu stopped walking and turned to me. "When you go back to America, do not forget us," he said. "You must tell our story to your people."

I knew what he was talking about. This was my second month in Kigoma. I had seen the piles of smoldering trash lying everywhere. Every day, children wearing tattered clothing ran past me, barefoot in the dusty streets. The surrounding hills had long ago been deforested for wood for fuel and building materials.

The local water was contaminated, and many people got sick throughout the year. I can personally vouch for this. In my short time there, I contracted the giardia parasite that gave me painful bloating, fevers and constant diarrhea for three weeks. On top of that, my colleague from the nearby Congo picked up typhoid fever, and my Tanzanian supervisor came down with amoebic dysentery. We had all been drinking bottled water, but somehow we still ended up getting very sick. Most residents in the community cannot afford the luxury of bottled water, and even those that manage to build up some degree of resistance, often suffer from these and other preventable diseases.

Take this to a global scale: bad water (or lack of water) ranks as one of the top causes of childhood death. It is estimated that about five to six thousand children die every day from easily preventable waterborne diseases.[1] That's about one child every fifteen seconds. How can conditions like this still exist today?

There are many factors to take into account in the Kigoma situation. The poorly funded education system and frequent refugee influxes from neighboring war zones are two concerns. In essence, though, many of the problems have environmental roots. Natural resources are depleted, and pollution from outside sources affects the residents' health.

Whether it is because of deforestation and erosion, poor water resources, dwindling fish catches or unsanitary waste disposal, environmental degradation is one of the leading factors that keep the people of Kigoma impoverished. These people depend directly on their local environment for survival, and their natural resource base is fast disappearing.

This situation is just a glimpse of what is going on throughout the world. Stories and statistics of communities suffering from environmental disasters are all over the news. During my two short months in Tanzania, however, these stories and statistics became personal. I could not treat them dispassionately, as if they were mere numbers in a newspaper article.

The people had names, faces and voices. They were my brother, my sister, my mother and my father. They held my hand and called me by name.

Walking along the road, hand in hand with this respected professor and brother in Christ, I made a decision: I would share his story—their story—when I came back home to the United States. I would not sit back and let the comforts of the American Dream insulate me from the rest of the world. No, not when so many of my local and global neighbors lack the most basic resources I take for granted. Not when there is an environmental crisis brought on in large part by our unsustainable lifestyle of overconsumption. Not when there is so much that I—that we as the church—can do to help.

Many issues in life are confusing. This one is clear. Many concerns can wait until tomorrow. This one won't. Our planet is in crisis. Creation is groaning. Our neighbors are suffering. The time for Christians to take a stand is now.

Winds of Change

Jesus calls us to love our neighbor and to be good stewards of what he has made. For far too long, though, the Western church has been passive on the growing global concern for the earth. The good news is that this is changing.

All across the church, Christians are waking up to God's call to care for his besieged creation and to love the poor who are suffering the most from environmental degradation. Not too long ago, Christian environmental activists were rare and were often viewed as part of a tree-hugging, granola-eating, fashion-insensitive, hygienically challenged, radical fringe. Now, however, creation care is regaining its rightful place as a central part of discipleship, and new waves of young Christians are taking up the call to help save this planet.

There is only one problem: we struggle to know how.

Of course, we do know some things. We know what is going wrong, and we understand much of the science behind it. We know what needs to be done, and we have the technical expertise to do it. Some individuals already implement this knowledge and practice elements of sound environmental living. We have memorized the mantra: reduce, reuse, recycle. But this is not enough.

What more can we do?

The Next Step

We need to think bigger . . . much bigger. All the science in the world and heroic individual effort are of limited good until we understand how to engage one another and work toward affecting change together.

It has taken masses of people to deplete the world's fisheries, overdraw the underground aquifers, clear-cut the rainforests and even modify the climate. It will also take the masses to turn this unsustainable trend around.

As individuals, this generation increasingly affirms that the earth is in crisis and that creation care is a priority for Christians. Time is running out. Changing light bulbs is a crucial first step, but we must not stop there. It is time to take the next step; it is time to join together in action.

My parents live in Massachusetts. Almost every year, a pod of pilot whales beaches on Cape Cod. Imagine an early-morning jogger out on the beach, coming across thirty to fifty of these small whales stranded in the shallows. They flop their tails in vain as the receding tide exposes even more of their drying bodies. The jogger rushes toward the nearest whale and uses his shirt as a sponge to squeeze life-saving water over its shuddering body. He tries to push, but there is no way his 160 pounds is going to budge a three-ton beached whale.

A passerby stops and skeptically asks the jogger what real difference he will make, gesturing at all the other dying whales for emphasis. As the jogger gently scoops another handful of refreshing water over his whale, he replies, "I'm making a difference to this one."

Have you heard this story before? Perhaps there were thousands of stranded starfish in place of the pod of whales.[2] Regardless, it is an important story for our situation today. There is some truth to what the jogger says. He is making a difference to that whale. Granted, he may not even save its life in the end, but he is certainly making far more of a difference than the skeptic passing by.

But the skeptic makes a good point. If success is defined by bringing the whales back into deeper water, the situation reeks of failure (and rotting whales).

But he should not stop there. What would happen if, instead of gawking in passivity, the passerby called his family to help? What if, in turn, others on the beach joined in the effort and alerted the news media? And they ran the story, and local residents poured down to help.

Soon the beach would be lined with hundreds of people working together to keep the whales from drying out. They would call in boats and coax the whales, one by one, out into open water.

This really happens whenever a pod beaches on the Cape.

Individually, we might make a modest difference at best, or we might make no difference at all. But together, we can conquer far greater challenges.

Making the Connection

The environmental crisis is every bit as urgent, and infinitely larger, than a pod of whales stranded on a beach. We are facing resource shortages in every sector across the globe. With increasing populations demanding more resources per capita, and a growing disparity between the rich and the poor, we are quickly running out of food, water, land and even clean air. Epidemics of afflictions such as SARS, the bird flu and West Nile virus are ever on the verge of emerging, modern medicine notwithstanding. Wars fought over oil today will be fought over water tomorrow. And in a dramatic abdication of our leadership role as stewards, our patterns of consumption have brought on the next great extinction period.

This is no longer alarmism; it has become reality. In what was previously unthinkable, the human race is now causing more change to the state of the earth than any other natural process.[3] Perhaps it is about time we changed.

Every personal action toward a greener lifestyle counts. The smallest of our contributions matters to God, and we should never judge its significance by how effective it appears to us in the grand scheme of things. God is pleased when we take personal steps to live intentionally, and individual changes, such as taking shorter showers or composting table scraps, really do save water and waste. Yet they are also only the beginning.

Environmental stewardship starts but does not stop at the individual level. God created us as unique individuals, but he also calls us together as the church. We need to bring others onboard to work together to truly make a difference on a broad scale. Richard Foster makes this point in his classic work *Freedom of Simplicity* when he writes, "While individual effort is good, it is always limited. There are things that we can do together that we cannot possibly do alone. God has so arranged human life that we are dependent upon one another to come into all that he desires of us." [4]

Therefore, what we really need is a movement of creation care efforts on every campus, in every church and across each community, a movement that will reimagine every aspect of our lives and communities in light of how God created us to live with each other on his earth. This will increase our effectiveness in raising awareness and encouraging others to personal action. Beyond that, it will mobilize us to make the collective changes that would have been unattainable on our own.

The good news is that this movement is underway and spreading rapidly. Communities of Christians all over the United States, Europe and around the world are taking on some of our most pressing environmental and social concerns and, because they are tackling them together, they are making a compelling difference.

Why This Book?

The purpose of this book is to share the good news of this growing creation care movement and to invite you to join in.

I am writing this as a recent college graduate who first got involved in creation care on my campus as a freshman and am now working with campuses, churches and communities around the country to initiate new local movements and support existing ones.

This book comes out of these experiences. Very little—if anything—in these pages is truly original. Rather than reinvent the wheel, my goal is to integrate what I have learned from others along with on-the-ground stories from creation care initiatives.

I do this in three parts. The first section ("Reality Check") sets a foundation for understanding the current environmental crisis, identifying its underlying causes and proposing solutions. The second section ("Changing Our Communities") explores stories about and strategies from the creative ways communities of Christians are bringing about hopeful change. The final section ("A Bigger Vision") is about how our local efforts fit into the larger movement and those outside the church.

As a young adult, I'm intentionally writing this to my fellow classmates, activists and other Christians in our Millennial Generation; this is the audience I am part of and relate most naturally to. At the same time, I hope this will also be encouraging and helpful to those who are not from our generation and those who make no claim to follow Jesus Christ.

Will You Join Us?
Now is a momentous time for the church and for our generation. The fight to save the planet involves all of us, and we are beyond the point where half measures and partial fixes will be enough.

Those who own Hummers or private jets are not solely responsible for our environmental crisis; we all share in the blame together. Some of us have lighter environmental footprints than others, but we all impact the planet at some level. Likewise, saving the planet is not just the job of the Nobel Prize–winning scientists; we all share in the responsibility. All of us need to pursue becoming less of the problem and more of the solution.

Yet no one person is going to fix these problems alone. The church is a body, and we are called to unity for good reason. We need each other and, somehow, we need to come together.

The difficulties we face are great, but therefore so are the opportunities. Winston Churchill, Great Britain's prime minister during World War II, had some outstanding strengths but also many weaknesses (like the rest of us). He was a courageous and wise leader during a time of great danger, when the advancing Nazi army threatened the very existence of Britain. In the face of overwhelming challenges, Churchill was able to rally his nation to a vision of hope and action instead of giving in to fear and despair.

Two keys to his success were his lasting determination and his aggressively hopeful outlook. As he said so well, "A pessimist sees the difficulty in every opportunity; an optimist sees the opportunity in every difficulty."

The eyes of the world are on the church, and the eyes of the church are on our generation. We have the chance to make a real difference here and to leave a lasting legacy that will point others toward Christ. I have great hope that we will seize this opportunity together.

Part 1

Reality Check

1

Incompatible Foolishness
Our Plan for the World vs. God's

The growing possibility of our destroying ourselves and the world with our own neglect and excess is tragic and very real.

Billy Graham, *Approaching Hoofbeats,* 1983

Drunken people should not go swimming.

I was in Corpus Christi, Texas, during the summer of my sophomore year to work on a government-funded fisheries research project, and I often spent weekends cooling off at a nearby beach.

While lying on the sand relaxing one Saturday, I noticed a commotion out in the surf. An older man, perhaps in his late fifties, was thrashing wildly in deeper water as a woman of comparable age struggled to tow him toward the beach. Not only was he flailing, he was also cussing up quite a storm. When the water was about knee deep, the woman let go of him so that she could catch her breath enough to start yelling back, but without her steadying grip, he promptly rolled face forward into the surf. Not quite sure what was going on, I ran down to see if they needed help.

The man had clearly been drinking too much and had apparently decided to go for a swim when his wife (the woman) was not paying attention. He made it just far enough to be in over his head before getting exhausted and going under. Providentially, his wife noticed what was happening at this point and jumped in to save him. Once they got into shallower water, however, he forgot to be grateful and instead was outraged that she wanted him to get out of the water.

As he continued to alternate between cussing and choking on seawater, his wife and I dragged him by the arms into a sitting position on the beach, where a concerned crowd had gathered. She kept thanking me for the little help I had given, to which he angrily declared that there was no problem and that he didn't need any help. "I'm a trained fighter," he continued to rave almost incoherently, "and you're lucky I didn't just kill you with a single judo chop to the neck!" Snickers ran through the crowd at this assertion, and the drunken man looked ready to start cussing again, but instead, as he opened his mouth, his eyes rolled and he passed out face-first in the sand.

Lesson number one: drunken people think they know better; they do not. Lesson number two: drunken people think they are in control; they are not. Lesson number three: it's a bad idea—even a dangerous one—to get drunk.

Our Wisdom

As a global society, we have become drunk on our own perceived power and wisdom. We pride ourselves for being civilized, educated, technologically advanced and increasingly developed. It is undeniable that we now know more about the intricacies of the world (we have even mapped the whole human genome), have developed more powerful tools (like commercialized air travel, cellular technology and precision-guided missiles) and are harnessing more of nature's productivity and stored energy (through intensive farming, high-tech fishing and fossil-fuel mining) than at any other point in human history.

Yes, we are the most educated and most advanced generation yet to live on this planet. But being smarter does not make us wiser. And being more advanced does not mean we are more moral.

In spite of all our progress, we have lost the ability to live well and live sustainably. The wisdom of the world consistently promotes the seven deadly sins over the Ten Commandments and the Beatitudes. We are promised fulfillment through the false gods of individualism, narcissism and consumerism. Our culture entices us to pursue personal pleasure by chasing after the hottest idols and buying the latest stuff, and the more we consume, the more intoxicated we become.

In our drunken state, we fail to realize and respect our limitations and those of the planet by continuing to ratchet up unsustainable rates of population growth, resource consumption and waste production. The result is that we have waded over our heads into troubled waters, stressing our global society and the planet beyond what it can bear. And we are starting to drown.

The claim that we are drowning is a strong assertion, but it also appears to be a fair one. Our global environment is in increasingly bad shape by almost all measures, even though some things such as forest cover and overall air and water quality have gotten better in parts of the developed world. Here are some snapshots:

- Over 1 billion people lack an adequate supply of water today, and this is projected to rise to 1.8 billion by 2025.

- Overall fish stocks are in their worst state yet, with three quarters of marine fisheries exploited unsustainably. The hardest-hit fisheries include previously ubiquitous species such as Atlantic cod and Pacific salmon.

- Other food production (through agriculture and livestock farming) is being stretched to the limit, and arable land is being lost on a constant basis, especially in Africa. As a result, food costs are rising and have resulted in the beginnings of a global food crisis.

- Developed nations may be getting cleaner, but that's largely because they are "exporting" pollution to the developing world, where exposure to these pollutants is responsible for 20 percent of human disease.

- An estimated 60 percent of all ecosystems are degraded and unsustainably used.[1]

- Biodiversity loss is accelerating rapidly. Between a quarter and a third of all wildlife has disappeared since 1970, and a full third of all amphibians are threatened with extinction.[2]

- Deforestation continues at an estimated rate of 13 million hectares (32 million acres) a year, with most of it occurring in the tropics to make way for cattle grazing, soybean farming and oil palm plantations.[3]

- The evidence for human-caused climate change continues to grow, and predictions of sea-level rise and extreme weather events become more serious given the acceleration of melting ice at the poles.[4]

- About 1 billion people live on less than one U.S. dollar a day and at least 2.6 billion (or 40 percent of the world population) live on under two dollars a day. These poorest of the poor are the most vulnerable to the effects of environmental degradation and climate change—effects that are being felt even now.[5]

It is clear that we are in a crisis and desperately need some solutions. Developing more advanced technology is ultimately not going to be the easy answer that many are hoping for. For one, we already know and have what we need to make the world a much better place. Technology is merely a tool; it can be either helpful or harmful, depending on whose hands it is in. In the hands of a drunk, a car is a murder weapon instead of a blessing; in the hands of a drunken society, and in spite of some very good intentions, our best technology has consistently been co-opted to fight wars and exploit the earth instead of save lives and protect the planet.

Better technology is also not the right solution because the problem is not primarily a technical one.[6] Instead, this is inherently a spiritual problem—the world is intoxicated on sin. A leading environmentalist and academician is reported to have confessed to a group of Christian leaders and scientists in 2007, "I used to think that the three greatest problems in the world were pollution, species extinction, and climate change. Now, I realize that they are pride, greed, and apathy; and scientists do not have the answers to these."[7]

This diagnosis is neither new nor groundbreaking. It is a problem as old as the Garden of Eden, when the original human pair first disobeyed the Creator, favoring their wisdom and pursuing their plan over his. Ever since, human history has been replete with the same basic story line of God's offering to rescue us back to the firm ground of his plan and of humans' stubbornly reasserting our free will to do what we want and so reinforcing our bondage to sin, which always leads to death (see Rom 1:21-32; 6:15-18).

Yet we still find good reason to hope; not everything is completely bad. Yes, humanity is fallen and, yes, the earth has been cursed. But humans are still created in God's image, and the earth still reflects his glory. There is enough virtue and progress around us and throughout history to reassure us that God has not given up on his creation.

Consider the international outpouring of aid that came from both Christian and non-Christian sources immediately after tsunamis ravaged parts of Asia in December 2004. Rejoice that, while the church was largely silent about issues of creation care, many non-Christians stepped up to give leadership in what has now developed into a robust global environmental movement.

The point I want to make is not that all has been lost, but rather that the overall trajectory of humanity apart from God is tragic and suicidal.[8]

Genesis tells us that Eve and then Adam ate the forbidden fruit in the Garden of Eden because it looked pleasing to the eye and was desirable for gaining wisdom. But look where our "wisdom" has gotten us so far. Like a drunken person, the world thinks it knows better, but it does not; the world thinks it is in control, but it is not. As a result, we have become dangerous not only to ourselves but to the whole creation.

Our prevailing plan for ourselves and this planet is not working. We need another way.

God's Wisdom

Creation care ministry Restoring Eden puts out a bumper sticker that reads, "God's original plan was to hang out in a garden with some naked vegetarians." More than just being catchy, this statement effectively makes the point that things were created to be very different. God has another plan for the world besides the broken reality we see around us, and he is enacting this plan even now.

God's alternative vision to our madness—a vision extending to all domains of life—is one of shalom, and his mission is the restoration of this shalom. This is the heart of our message.

Shalom is the Hebrew word for peace. Meaning more than simply the absence of conflict, however, it is about right relationships between God and everything else, where wholeness and flourishing occurs without opposition. Such shalom was present in the Garden of Eden, and its complete restoration is what we eagerly anticipate in the kingdom of God.

In the words of author Mark Gornik, "Shalom is God putting back together a broken world. . . . Shalom is not just the wolf and the lamb co-existing but the wolf and the lamb finding their rest in one another (Isaiah 11:6-7; 65:25). Shalom is more than physical safety for the child playing near the cobra's nest; it is the child and the cobra successfully playing together."[9]

In Genesis 3 we read the tragic account of how shalom was originally lost and relationships were fractured through the fall of humanity and the subsequent curse on creation. Ever since that point, God has been in the business of reconciling all relationships to himself. This mission was fulfilled in the life, death and resurrection of Christ, and will culminate when he returns in glory.

Because shalom was lost from all of creation, it must now be restored to all creation, human and nonhuman. Right relationships must be restored between God and us, within our relationship to ourselves, between us and each other, between us and nature, and within nature itself.

Bad or inappropriate relationships exist because there are injustices. A key part of restoring these broken relationships to wholeness is fixing the injustices that perpetuate them; there can be no peace without justice. This is why creation care is also inherently a justice issue. Injustices have been committed against God, the earth and one another, and these wrongs must be righted if there is to be any true and lasting shalom.

Not too long ago I got an e-mail from a missionary couple living on the Peruvian coast, asking for help dealing with the industrial pollution coming from fishmeal factories in their community. They describe a situation that lacks justice, peace and wholeness:

> An urgent issue is controlling the industrial pollution from the fishmeal factories. At the end of every "run" they flush their tanks with harsh chemicals and dump everything directly into the bay. Our local bay is almost barren of animal life. We especially notice the difference in invertebrates compared to the neighboring bays around us. Controlling this pollution is important for protecting

the health and integrity of our community. However, there would be strong financial and political elements opposing it. Perú already has laws prohibiting this pollution, but corruption effectively cancels enforcement.[10]

Our deep brokenness and desperate need for reconciliation are glaringly apparent in environmental issues like this.

In this case, those responsible for the fishmeal factory are unjustly degrading the environment, harming the community and ultimately pursuing material profits over God (it is cheaper not to properly dispose of their industrial waste, even though it is also wrong). All three levels of human relationships—with God, one another and creation—are being violated. This is not how God intends us to live, and there can be no shalom under these circumstances. As Francis Schaeffer wrote, "If I am going to be in the right relationship with God, I should treat the things he has made in the same way he treats them."[11] We must value what God values and so treat this good creation in a way that honors him as the Creator.

If we take this one step further, we get back to the root cause of the environmental crisis because, as the Christian theologian Cornelius Plantinga Jr. points out, whatever opposes God's intentions and violates his shalom is sin.[12] This was true when Eve and Adam ate the forbidden fruit, and it is true of bad environmental stewardship today. In other words, dumping untreated toxic waste into a bay in Peru is not just bad because it breaks the law; it is also sinful because it works against God's design and desire for the world.

All Things

When we think of the need for shalom in the world, it is easy to think first and mainly of human concerns, such as the war in Iraq, Sudan's Darfur crisis and the Israeli-Palestinian conflict. We rarely think of "environmental issues" like pollution, deforestation and a scarcity of water. But Jesus Christ is the Lord of all, and he is bringing peace and reconciliation to all levels of relationships through his blood shed on the cross:

He is the image of the invisible God, the firstborn over all creation.
For by him all things were created: things in heaven and on earth,
visible and invisible, whether thrones or powers or rulers or
authorities; all things were created by him and for him. He is
before all things, and in him all things hold together. . . . For God
was pleased to have all his fullness dwell in him, and through him
to reconcile to himself all things, whether things on earth or things
in heaven, by making peace through his blood, shed on the cross.
(Col 1:15-17, 19-20)

We serve a big God who is in the business of reconciling, through
Christ, the entire created order back to his shalom. Nothing less.
Working for world peace does not mean focusing first on human wars
and thinking about "the rest" later. Everything needs reconciliation and,
in God's plan, everything gets it together.

Moreover, if we were to focus all our efforts on eradicating wars, there
would be no human peace—no right relationships within humanity
itself—unless the environment were also taken into account in the
peacemaking process.

The Darfur conflict in Sudan is a tragic example of this
interconnectedness of environmental issues with peace and the
interdependence of sustainability and societal well-being. Since 2003,
reports of horrendous atrocities have poured out of the troubled Darfur
region: over 200,000 people dead, thousands raped, children forced to
fight as soldiers, two million residents displaced. The appalling statistics
increase. Meanwhile, the Sudanese government has been defiantly
complicit in the violence, and the international community has been
characteristically weak in its response. Peace is nowhere to be found.

Watching and reading about this war with growing sadness and
frustration, I always assumed it was an ethnic conflict, which it is. But I
was surprised to find out just how large a role environmental issues play.
During 2007, many of the major news networks reported on the potential
discovery of a huge underground lake in the Darfur region. The great
excitement around this discovery was that there was hope it could help
end the war.

Dispatch: Jonathan Kindberg, M.A. candidate (2009), Wheaton College Graduate School

Shalom and the Holy Land

Israel, where *shalom* is used for both greetings and farewells, has seen little shalom either in its social or in its environmental contexts over the past sixty years. This past summer, I saw firsthand what this lack of peace entails, for both land and people.

For three months I lived in a Palestinian refugee camp in the occupied West Bank. When I arrived, the camp was in the midst of a water cut that had already lasted two weeks. The Israeli government controls water in Palestinian refugee camps, and cuts are frequent during the hot summer months. Every Palestinian home has a set of reserve tanks on its roof. These are full when there is water. But when the water supply is cut, the tanks gradually empty until there is simply no more water.

During my stay, Israelis celebrated forty years of the reunification of Jerusalem while Palestinians mourned forty years of oppression, occupation and loss of their land and water. In the West Bank, story after story and scene after scene of suffering assailed me. I witnessed haunting rows of stumps—all that remained of hundred-year-old olive trees that the Israeli military had cut down to crush morale in the territories. I walked on the future path of another part of the "separation barrier," a wall that separates thousands of farmers from their fields and has destroyed thousands of hectares of arable land. I listened to the stories of Palestinian youth who can't find enough water to wash their face in the morning, while they watch Israeli settlers play in swimming pools nearby.

Palestinians are considered the most water-deprived

people in the Middle East.[a] According to World Vision, they receive only 33 to 40 percent of average water requirements set by the World Health Organization.[b] The reason for this shortage is not a lack of water, but a lack of fair distribution. Israel monopolizes the aquifers underlying the West Bank and uses 95 percent for itself, leaving the remaining 5 percent for Palestinian use.[c]

Simon Awad is a Palestinian Christian and the executive director of the Environmental Education Center of the Evangelical Lutheran Church. This center, based in the West Bank, actively works for environmental justice. For Simon, "the environmental situation in Palestine is damaged because there is no control of their own land." He states that the environment "is a gift of God that we should save for the next generation." In the West Bank, where politics, power and the environment collide, the occupation stands as a barrier to shalom, for both the land and the people.

[a]Harald D. Frederiksen, "A Proposal: Return Palestinian Water Rights If Not Land," *Middle East Policy* 2, no. 1 (Spring 2005): 72-78.
[b]"Water for Life in the West Bank," World Vision (November 8, 2006) <www.worldvision.org.uk/server/php?show=nav.883>.
[c]Frederiksen, "A Proposal," p. 72.

At the root of this conflict is competition for natural resources such as water and land—made worse by drought and desertification—between Arab nomads and black African farmers. Ban Ki-Moon, secretary-general of the United Nations, wrote, "Darfur's violence began with the onset of a decades-long drought. Farmers and herders came into conflict over land and water. If this root problem is not addressed—if the challenges of poverty alleviation, environmental stewardship and the control of climate change are not tied together—any solutions we propose in Darfur will at best be a temporary Band-Aid."[13]

In this tragic example, we see that peacemaking is about more than just ethnic reconciliation and the laying down of arms. It's also about environmental justice and stewardship of natural resources. This is the main point in the secretary-general's article: "The basic building block of peace and security for all peoples is economic and social security, anchored in sustainable development. It is a key to all problems. Why? Because it allows us to address all the great issues—poverty, climate, wenvironment and political stability—as parts of a whole."[14] When the planet is not at peace, people are not at peace either.

Time to Choose

It boils down to two opposing visions: the wisdom of the world and the wisdom of God. We have to choose which one to live by.

We live in a world that is trapped in idolatry, lured by the siren calls of materialism, individualism and narcissism, and pursuing almost every other voice except God's. We, along with the planet, are paying the price for our disregard of how life was originally created to flourish.

We even live in a church that can be so enmeshed with the dominant culture that the two are hard to tell apart. Peter Harris, the founder of A Rocha, speaks of this problem:

> While environmental people are worried about genetically modified organisms, we Christians should be worried about whether we belong to a genetically modified church. I worry that the DNA of the deeply materialistic and individualistic societies that we live in has become so patched into our reading of what it means to be a Christian that we are not talking the biblical gospel any longer.[15]

Yet God is still calling to us, though it can sometimes be hard to hear his voice in our cluttered lives. He offers a vision of shalom that is neither practical nor trendy, but it is both timeless and true. By following him, we find peace, redemption and healing for ourselves and for the world around us. His plan gives us answers to the problems we have created— environmental and otherwise—and shows that there is a better and more sustainable way to live.

Uplink: Will Samson, author of *Justice in the Burbs*

There's an old saying in advertising: you should be willing to eat your own dog food. If you sell a product to others, you should believe in it enough to use it yourself. This has always been the call of the gospel. Jesus didn't tell us to go far and wide speaking *about* the cross. No, he told us to *take up* our cross and follow him—to act on what we believe.

But I often get hung up at about this point, the place where I am supposed to step out and walk my talk. It all seems a bit too bold, a bit too audacious. Could it really matter?

In our community we are planting a garden at the cross streets between a white neighborhood and a black neighborhood, where there have been racial tensions for more than one hundred years. What kind of people would be bold enough to think that a community garden could heal divisions and to believe that God could help change a city through tomatoes and Brussels sprouts?

When I work in Appalachia, seeking to improve conditions for those affected by mountaintop-removal mining, it seems nothing short of crazy to hope that my presence—the presence of a Yankee raised far from the hills of eastern Kentucky—could bring healing among a southern rural people who have been struggling with poverty for generations. This is a people whose economic conditions have only grown worse as their resources have been taken and sold,

transferring the profits to out-of-state corporations while they are left to live with the coal sludge and the devastating air pollution. Is it rash—or, worse yet, careless—to believe my work there will make any difference? Things in Appalachia have been getting worse for more years than anyone can count. What kind of boldness could keep me going back?

How about when I perform more basic tasks, like recycling, switching to compact fluorescent bulbs, composting or shopping for local meat and produce? Can I really make a difference? Isn't the problem much bigger than anything I could help solve?

And then I remember the story that I am a part of, a story that started with Abram and his wife, Sarai. Despite their advanced age, they were told they would have a son—and that son would start a new nation. Crazy.

I remember that I am part of a story about God incarnate, whose miracles were all, save one (the cursing of the fig tree), about the restoration of creation—a king who, himself, would go beyond the point where everything was lost, only to claim the victory.

My mind moves through stories of the early Christian martyrs, so moved by Jesus that they risked life and limb to follow. Saints like Francis of Assisi were willing to follow Jesus' call to the rich young ruler, sell everything they had and follow him. And we know modern-day saints, like Matthew Sleeth and Shane Claiborne, who have bet it all on the bold and adventurous claim that we are colaborers with Christ, participating as the hands and feet of Jesus in restoring and redeeming the world for God.

And I begin to hope. Maybe I will not live to see the world perfected. We still exist in that space between what has been and what will be, the space where Paul reminds us that "all creation groans" as we wait for the earth and our bodies to be restored. But as I look back on all God has done and as I look around at all the God is doing, I realize I have the chance to participate with the King of creation, to get my hands dirty in the restoration of creation.

Now that's something I could believe in. And this is exactly what Ben is laying out in these pages. So, want to join us?

2

Prodigal Treehuggers
Our Place in God's Plan

Everyone is an environmentalist. We cannot live independently of the world
God has placed us in. We are intimately connected. By God.

Rob Bell, *Velvet Elvis: Repainting the Christian Faith*

Eric and Joanne Norregaard faced an unexpected problem: their compost
bin was running out of space.

Eric initially thought about swinging out to a nearby home-
improvement store to pick up some materials for the job. Looking
around the small yard, however, he and Joanne noticed the now-rusty
playground set that their two kids had played with years before (they
were now in high school). The ground under the set would make a good
place for a new compost pile. On a whim, they grabbed some tools,
dismantled part of the playground and reworked the pieces into a
functional, albeit less orthodox-looking, compost bin, complete with a
swing set.

The Norregaards lead a pretty average—and until recently, also
compost-free—suburban life. Along with their two kids, Katie and
Stephen, they live in a modest one-story home outside Chicago and are
part of the Wheaton Chinese Alliance Church (WCAC), where Eric serves
as the worship director. A couple of years earlier, WCAC had held a
special Sunday school series on creation care that really got the
Norregaards and other families thinking about their worldview and
lifestyle.

Before this series, the church as a whole had not thought much about
creation care or regarded it as a Christian concern. After the series,
however, and under the leadership of the pastoral staff and members of
the youth group, things slowly started to change. Recycling signs and
bins appeared one day, and leaders took turns emptying them. Staff

The Norregaard family by their compost pile. Photo by Ben Lowe.

streamlined the Sunday service bulletins from two pages to one, switched to recycled paper and included creation care themes in the songs and prayers. During worship services on warmer days, they even started turning off the lights in the sanctuary and opening the windows, both to use less energy and to help the congregation reconnect in a small way with the natural world.[1]

These may appear to be modest initial steps, but they signify a deep change in the hearts and minds of those involved. WCAC is similar to many traditional Chinese American churches in being relatively conservative and generally wary of hopping on perceived trends. Once they realized that God's mission of cosmic reconciliation includes all of creation, however, the congregation understood that caring for the environment is a biblical mandate, not just a popular trend. And if it is a biblical mandate, they needed to repent for ignoring it and start living it out a lot better.

Perhaps the costliest indicator of their growing commitment to this enlarged vision of shalom came two years after the creation care Sunday school series, when the missions committee and elder board agreed to contribute financially to A Rocha, the international Christian conservation organization I was serving through.

Eric and the pastoral staff were largely responsible for initiating these and other changes in how the congregation lives out their commitment to the inbreaking kingdom of God. These changes also go hand-in-hand with what congregants started doing at home. For instance, one of the pastors replaced his truck with a very fuel-efficient sedan, and the Norregaards started conserving energy and composting in their backyard. Eric e-mailed me an update recently:

> Since the creation care seminar series, our family of four switched our home lighting to CFL bulbs, replaced our washing machine with a high-efficiency unit, and began composting. Our electric consumption dropped to under 300 kWh a month, we found ourselves generating only one can of garbage every two or three weeks instead of one to two cans every week, and a full can of trash weighs much less now without all the heavy food waste. For us, these are small steps toward living with more gratitude to God for the world He has entrusted to our care.[2]

The Norregaards and WCAC may think they are taking only small steps, but they are also setting an inspiring example for me and many others. As they take a firm stance against the ways of the world to embrace more fully the wisdom of God, they are recovering a biblically based vision for living more simply and compassionately toward all creation.

Socrates said, "The unexamined life is not worth living," and he makes an important point for us today. Overstimulated, overbooked, overcaffeinated and overwhelmed, we live in a hectic world that is far too busy about itself. I find it easy to get sucked into the madness of continually racing through my schedules, inboxes and to-do lists, rarely slowing down enough to consider where I'm headed in such a rush.

As the Norregaards and WCAC have found, however, it is worth making the effort to take a thorough and sincere look at how much we are living for God and his kingdom of shalom, and how much we have wandered off to live for ourselves and our earthly idols.

Coming Back

The parable of the prodigal son is one of my favorites (see Lk 15:11-32). There were two young men who lived a life of privilege in the home of their wealthy, landowning father. The younger son was not content, however. He wanted to do his own thing and so convinced his father to give him his share of the estate right away. Taking the inheritance, he traveled far away from home to party it up and irresponsibly burned through everything he had.

This wayward son hit rock bottom and remembered how much better life used to be back home with his family. He longed to return but realized how shamefully he had acted and how senselessly he had squandered his father's blessings. Eventually, out of desperation, he returned in disgrace with the hope that his dad would show pity and hire him on as a servant. We know how the story ends:

> But while he was still a long way off, his father saw him and was filled with compassion for him; he ran to his son, threw his arms around him and kissed him. The son said to him, "Father, I have sinned against heaven and against you. I am no longer worthy to be called your son." But the father said to his servants, "Quick! Bring the best robe and put it on him. Put a ring on his finger and sandals on his feet. Bring the fattened calf and kill it. Let's have a feast and celebrate. For this son of mine was dead and is alive again; he was lost and is found." (Lk 15:20-24)

Jesus shared this parable as a moving testimony of grace and redemption for all of us who have wandered from God's presence and squandered his blessings, but in desperation have realized our mistakes and are returning in brokenness and repentance. It is a hopeful story of great love and salvation.

It is also a story with many uncanny parallels to our situation today. We must be careful about reading our own agenda into the Bible and drawing out points that were never intended—in effect making us the ventriloquist and God our proverbial dummy (as my theologian father would put it). But where the plot overlaps and the principles are applicable, we stand to learn the lessons from this parable and take its promises to heart.

Consider this: We are created by God to be his children in the household that is his kingdom. He also created all manner of abundant life and blessed us with plentiful resources. We really have life made.

But, instead of being grateful stewards, we have spurned God and his divine plan. As we saw in chapter one, we have taken our inheritance—the earth—in our own hands and squandered it at alarming rates on our own wants. Faced by environmental crises on every side and all around the globe, we are awakening to a desperate reality: we have wandered far from God's good intentions for us and for the world. We are hurting and have nowhere else to turn. It is time to remember our Father God. It is time to go back home.

The church today, like the prodigal son, is returning for imperfect reasons. The prodigal did not want to head home because he had wronged his father, but because he was hoping for a better life again. Likewise, the trigger for our recovery of a vision of environmental stewardship today is not foremost because we have been drifting from God, but because we can no longer ignore our ailing environment and are worried for our well-being. It starts out as a selfish reason but, as with the son, we learn to take on a position of true humility and repentance. We have no right to expect God to welcome us back to our old place. All we can do is plead for mercy from a heavenly Father who has every right to be disappointed and angry.

Instead, however, when God sees us returning, he is joyful and full of grace. It is an astounding response. I believe that as Christians turn back in true repentance for the way we have often abused creation and each other for selfish ends, God welcomes us back with open arms of forgiveness and celebration. He reconciles us to his household, and we are restored to our original role as adopted sons and daughters in his kingdom of shalom.

Finding Our Place

What does it mean to live as children of God, and what is our role in his kingdom?

Recently, during a youth group lesson on environmental stewardship, a student named Josh read to us from Genesis 1. As he read about the creation of the plants and then of the various kinds of animals, he stopped abruptly and exclaimed, "There are so many 'according to their kinds' in this passage!" And he was right. None of us in the room had paid much attention to this, but in the two verses that describe the creation of plants, the phrase "according to their kinds" is used three times (vv. 11-12). In the five verses that describe the creation of all the animals, this same phrase is repeated a full seven times (vv. 20-25). The author drives home the point here that all living creatures were made according to their kinds.

Well, all creatures except one. The next verse moves on to the creation of humans, but instead of being created according to *our* kind, the text reveals that we are made in God's image and likeness—*God's* kind. Just in case there is any confusion about whether this is intentional, it is repeated three times within two verses (vv. 26-27).

This is an immense honor for us, and the implication of this distinction immediately follows in verse 28: we are created in God's image to rule and have dominion over his creation.[3] This does not mean—though it has often been misinterpreted to suggest—that humans get to do whatever we want and selfishly consume the rest of creation as if it were made for and belongs to us. The Scriptures are clear that creation was made for God (see Col 1:16) and still belongs to God (see Ps 24:1). We are, however, given great authority to serve as his stewards, representing him and working for his purposes in the created order.

Stewards do not ultimately own the property they care for, but are empowered to make intelligent decisions on behalf of the actual owner that would best reflect his or her wishes. In this case, we are also given the privilege of using the fruitfulness of creation responsibly for our own sustenance and enjoyment.

Our role as stewards is reinforced in Genesis 2:15, which says that God put humans in the Garden of Eden "to work it and take care of it." We certainly do not have a license to trash the good creation. Instead, God calls us to bear his image to the rest of creation and to rule and subdue it as his stewards in the same way he rules over us—with firmness and justice but also with gentleness, grace, compassion and creativity.

This is our original role in creation and the first commission God gives humans. In addition, Jesus strongly reinforces Old Testament teachings that the two greatest commandments are to love God and to love our neighbor as ourselves. We cannot love God fully unless we also love what he has made, and we cannot separate loving our neighbor from caring for the natural resources we all depend on to survive.

A Calling for All of Us

As Christians, our original role as stewards also entails a calling to the ministry of reconciliation (see 2 Cor 5:11-21). Our vision should be in line with God's vision, and our mission should likewise be in line with his. Working in partnership with the Holy Spirit and alongside the exalted Jesus Christ, we are called to pursue God's cause of restoring all levels of relationships back to his shalom. As Christian philosopher Nicholas Wolterstorff puts it,

> Shalom is both God's cause in the world and our human calling. Even though the full incursion of shalom into our history will be divine gift and not merely human achievement, even though its episodic incursion into our lives now also has a dimension of divine gift, nonetheless it is shalom that we are to work and struggle for. We are not to stand around, hands folded, waiting for shalom to arrive. We are workers in God's cause, his peace-workers. The *missio Dei* is our mission.[4]

While it is important that we are good stewards of all that God has placed in our care (including the environment, time, money, our bodies and much more), Wolterstorff makes the important point that we also are to be active participants in the grand process of reconciliation, even as we are also its recipients.

This process of reconciliation involves restoring the various broken relationships back to their original wholeness. There is a lot that we must depend on God to set right—and we are told that his Spirit is at work here in mysterious ways—but there are still significant aspects to the ministry of reconciliation that he empowers us to work on right now. For instance, we see great value in developing more wholesome relationships with each other and a healthier understanding of our own selves—two of the fractured relationships that resulted from the Fall. We know that neither ourselves nor our relationships with each other will be perfected on our own. Yet with God's help, we can keep them moving in the right direction (entire disciplines, such as psychology and counseling, are geared toward that end). Similarly, while we will never restore shalom to this planet on our own, we can still make good progress toward recovering our relationship to creation as its divinely appointed stewards.

How does this apply to our lives?

The first answer is that there is no one answer. "Calling" is a multifaceted concept. Some of us will be called to specifically address environmental issues as a full-time vocation. My undergraduate major at Wheaton College was environmental biology, and I work as a community organizer in the creation care movement. One of my classmates now works at the Field Museum of Natural History in Chicago, another is pursuing a graduate degree in groundwater pollution, and yet another is working with the National Park Service in addressing human-bear conflicts.

Does this mean you should, like my classmates and me, become an environmental science major and prepare for a career in conservation? Not necessarily. We do need more Christians to get involved in environmental professions, but there are also many other needs in the world and many equally important callings from God.

Other causes, starting with spiritual lostness and including abortion, the HIV/AIDS crisis, human trafficking, immigration reform, substance abuse, the depression epidemic, religious persecution, gender issues, accessible education, nuclear proliferation and so much more, are inextricably interconnected and must all be reconciled in order to realize the fullness of God's shalom.

This, however, does not get any of us off the hook. Individuals can care deeply about the planet and take an active role in caring for it while not making it their primary focus. At a very basic level, we all consume resources—food, water, energy and raw materials for iPods—and otherwise impact the environment. In turn, the environment has an impact on each of us. This is an unavoidable fact of being alive.

Therefore, we are all called to be stewards of creation as we live out our lives on this earth. We are all called to love God and love our neighbor, and to continue moving from being part of the problem to being more of the solution. And, wherever we have wandered, we are called to remember God and return home.

Our common calling to creation care applies on both an individual and a corporate level. This is where our theology and worldview are translated into action, where our faith and what we have learned are integrated into how we live.

Four principles can help set a framework for how we "do" creation care. These principles are not my own; they have gelled as many pioneering individuals and communities have approached the practice of creation care over the years.

First, we start with repentance. We have sinned by failing to take good care of creation. *Sin* is not a popular word today, but it is a daily reality for us all. We begin to change by repenting, asking God to forgive us for the ways we have been poor stewards of the earth and to help us become more like him.

This is part of what the Wheaton Chinese Alliance Church does together. On the last week of every month, they use the Sunday school time for a churchwide prayer meeting in the gym. These prayer meetings do not always have a theme, but sometimes focus around certain issues, such as missions, poverty or, in this case, the state of God's creation. Sometimes it is easier to do something that feels practical, such as change a light bulb, than to pray for the environment. But praying is both practical and powerful. During the creation care prayer meeting at WCAC, the congregation spent a meaningful portion of time silently and then corporately confessing and asking forgiveness for how they had failed to be good stewards of the earth.

Second, we move toward doing less harm to the planet. This includes steps that countless households, campuses, businesses and churches are taking, such as reducing energy and water consumption, and cutting back on travel and shopping.

For instance, well over five hundred higher-education institutions have now signed onto the American College and University Presidents Climate Commitment (ACUPCC), including at least five Christian colleges: Eastern University (Pennsylvania), Goshen College (Indiana), Messiah College (Pennsylvania), Point Loma Nazarene University (California) and Whitworth College (Washington).[5] At the core of the ACUPCC is a commitment to become climate neutral (not negatively impacting the climate by emitting greenhouse gases) through a combination of conservation measures and offsetting the remaining pollution through reforestation projects and other efforts. It may sound impossible, but smaller schools, such as College of the Atlantic (Bar Harbor, Maine), have already done it, and larger universities, ranging from Cornell to Arizona State, are well on their way.

Third, we find ways to do more good. This could be by simply getting out to enjoy God's creation and praise him, starting a community garden, planting native trees, cleaning trash from streams or getting involved in local environmental efforts such as the annual Audubon Society Christmas Bird Count, which has been going since the winter of 1900 and now involves more than fifty thousand participants across North America.[6] One advantage here is that as we bless creation, it often ends up blessing us as well; as we take care of creation, it takes care of us.

Fourth, we celebrate together. There is an amazing, creative, fruitful world outside our walls and away from our air conditioning, but it's easy to become so distracted that we rarely appreciate it. It's well worth taking time to enjoy God's creation and praise him for the abundant life he faithfully sustains in and around us.

A Priority for the Church

Not only is creation care a calling for all of us, it has also become a priority issue that we as the church should focus attention and resources on. Here are three reasons why:

It is an urgent crisis. The most urgent, ear-piercing sound I have ever heard is the fire alarm in my old dorm room back at Wheaton. Every time that alarm went off, I jumped up and got out of the building right away . . . even if only to get away from the noise. Many times, it was a false alarm triggered as a prank by someone in another dorm. Once in a while, though, there was a real fire or smoke emergency that was worth evacuating for.

Today, the world's leading scientists have triggered an urgent alarm. And this is no prank. They have been poring over the data and monitoring trends carefully for years. They are the experts, and not only have they seen smoke—they have seen the fire.

In a fire alarm, everyone in the building has to evacuate. In this environmental alarm, we have no other planet to escape to. Our only option is to team up to put the fire out.

It is an overriding problem. Many environmental issues run deep enough that they must be addressed in order to solve other crises. The Darfur conflict is a good case in point. But even without active violence and warfare, communities cannot rise out of long-term poverty if their natural resources are depleted. International aid can pour in, but if it is not used to help restore the environment to a functioning state, the problems will return as soon as the aid stops.

Climate change is another example. It is important to provide good health services for many poor, low-lying areas around the world like Bangladesh and numerous islands in the Pacific. However, if global climate change causes sea levels to rise and cover these locations with water, good health care is not going to count for much anymore. A healthy planet is foundational for life to prosper.

It is full of low-hanging fruit. Low-hanging fruit on a tree is the first to get picked because it is within easy reach, compared with fruit up on higher branches. Similarly, if we want to make a difference in the world, it usually makes sense to start by making changes that are already within our reach. It can be challenging to know where and how to address many of the big issues out there. But the environment is certainly not one of them. Many steps are within our reach. This is largely because we all directly and consciously depend on and interact with the environment as part of everyday life. In this sense, we are automatically already involved: we drive cars filled with gas; use water to shower, flush, wash and drink; write or print on paper; turn on the lights and so on. Besides staying aware, donating money and praying—all of which are vital ways to contribute—there is also a host of practical steps we can take right away to make a difference (I'll talk more about some of these in chapter six).

Clear Messaging

If creation care is a calling for all of us and a priority for the church, it is important to understand our unique role and to be able to communicate the message of creation care and shalom to those around us. We need to be clear about what we believe and on the same page with what we are asking from one another if we hope to make good progress back toward God's plan. And there is not a moment to lose.

One of the perks of studying environmental science in college is that it qualifies you for many exciting jobs. My long-term passion is in marine biology, and in this field of study, it is important to learn how to scuba dive. It was for this reason that I found myself jumping into the cold waters of Boston Harbor one spring weekend, all suited up in layers of insulating neoprene.

On one of my training dives in Boston's poor water visibility, I was not paying close attention, and all of a sudden I realized my tank was almost out of air. I was thirty feet down and had barely a couple of breaths left, so I immediately started motioning to my dive buddy. I flipped my air-pressure gauge up to show him that I was empty, and his eyes got real big. One of the safety features in scuba diving is that everyone has a spare regulator (mouthpiece) to share in case of such an emergency. We also have specific sign language so we can communicate underwater in circumstances like this. Well, I panicked and forgot about the sign language, and my dive buddy froze and continued to just stare at me. Wondering why he was not offering me his alternate regulator, I reached out to grab it myself, causing him to panic and back away.

At this point, I was holding my last breath and getting ready for an emergency ascent. Then, out of the murkiness, someone reached over my shoulder and handed me a regulator. It was my instructor, who had been secretly watching over us from the shadows and had figured out what was going on. After a few gulps of blessed air, I regained my breath, and we made our way back to the surface.

As I think back, the lessons I learned underwater in Boston Harbor are very relevant here. Like running out of air on a dive, our situation is important and urgent; we need to understand it and then communicate it well.

When we communicate our message, we also need to be clear about what we expect one another to do about it. I figured out what was going on right before running out of air, but did not find the right way to communicate this message to my dive buddy. As a result, when I became desperate and grabbed for his alternate regulator, he reacted against me and backed away. Similarly, in our urgency to address environmental concerns, we can become too forward and aggressive, succeeding only in confusing people and scaring them away.

We have an important role to play in God's plan for his creation, and we need to spread this message clearly throughout the church. The amount of progress we make depends largely on whether or not, unlike my poor dive buddy, but like the Norregaard family, we respond with the right actions.

Uplink: Fred Van Dyke, Ph.D., Director of Environmental Studies Program, Wheaton College

A Transformational Vocation

Ben Lowe did not arrive at Wheaton College thinking about environmental studies as a major or the stewardship of the world's nonhuman creation as a vocation. The eldest son of missionary parents, Ben was thinking about how to find a way to help *people,* especially in developing countries, through holistic mission and ministry that would touch every part of their lives. Because of that interest in people and concern for the human condition, Ben originally planned to study in a major that would help him prepare for a career in overseas development, such as political science or international relations.

When he was drawn, perhaps surprisingly, to our work at Wheaton College in the program of environmental studies, I had the opportunity, and the obligation, of giving Ben a right understanding of this work in the classes he began to take with me. But classes are, in many ways, extremely artificial and unreal environments for preparation for a wider world. My job was not merely to communicate ideas to him and the other students. Ideas are an important part of our worldview and our own identity, but ideas alone do not form us into the kind of people we ought to be unless we take personal responsibility for the world's problems and the conditions that those ideas address. As

all my students soon learn, the greatest hurdle, and most challenging goal, of the college education is not simply to pass your classes and gain a degree. It is to attain the status of a colleague, to learn to work alongside others in a vocation and ministry of purpose and hope. One cannot complete that journey in only four years, but one can go a long way down the road if one knows which road to take.

Ben took the right road because he began to take personal responsibility for the state of the Wheaton College community in regard to its level of stewardship and care for God's earth. He began to recognize that the work and vocation we often call "environmental stewardship" or "creation care" is merely a part of God's greater ministry of reconciliation of the entire created order to himself, accomplished in the work of Jesus Christ, and the blood he shed on the cross to achieve it (see Col 1:15-20). As Ben began to realize that people need to be reconciled to God, to one another, to themselves and to the physical world around them, he began to understand why such a ministry could have a vocational calling on one's entire life. And somewhere along the way he stopped complaining about and blaming other people for the state of things at Wheaton College, or anywhere else for that matter. He realized that the actions that had to be taken, the work that had to be done, had to begin with him. This recognition is an enormous step toward maturity. When we blame others and make excuses, we twist the truth and fail to see ourselves or our surroundings as they really are.

The shalom Ben speaks of in this chapter begins with seeing ourselves as responsible agents of change in God's world, persons made in God's image and empowered by his Holy Spirit to create good, even in places where no good presently exists. When we see things this way, and act on what we see, we begin to work with God toward eternal and significant purposes that will affect every part of the created order. It was this perspective—daily growing and developing in Ben as he continued to work out his vocation at Wheaton College and all over the United States and the world in his summer employment and internships in environmental study and stewardship—that helped him learn how to communicate the message of an urgent crisis with a sense of peace and humility, not "grabbing at the regulator" as he did on that dive in Boston Harbor and driving people away, but communicating a message of shalom that all people can hear and receive.

The hope for the earth is God's determination not only to redeem it but also to include more and more people like Ben in that redemptive effort. They are passionate in knowing the urgency of the need, but at peace in God's power working within them for his glory and for the redemption of the earth. You will find this blend of urgency and peace in Ben, and in his words in this book. So keep reading. He has much yet to say.

3

From Insulation to Incarnation
The Journey Back to God's Plan

We cannot be all that God wants us to be without caring for the earth.

Rick Warren

Droughts? Famines? Deforestation? Species loss? We may be keenly aware of skyrocketing gas prices at the pump but, beyond that, it can be easy to feel removed from what is happening to our neighbors and the earth. Environmental issues are conversation topics that we pick up from the news, but they usually do not directly affect our day-to-day lives.

Of course, there are plenty of exceptions, and conditions can change all too quickly, as the residents of New Orleans experienced with Hurricane Katrina. However, the majority of us are quite disconnected from the land and isolated from each other and the impacts of our consumerist lifestyles.[1] This high degree of insulation helps shield us from reality and is a major underlying factor behind environmental degradation.

Reality Check

"I need nature, open space and peaceful nights. I will never choose to live in a city. It's just too dirty, congested and noisy." This used to be my answer when people asked me where I would like to live when I grew up.

But during the fall after graduating from college, I moved into a cheap apartment in Chicago with a few close friends. We had recently read *The Irresistible Revolution,* a book by a fellow activist named Shane Claiborne, and were challenged to explore what living simply and intentionally in an urban setting could look like.

Our apartment was next door to a bar in one of the city's most ethnically diverse neighborhoods. We shared the building with three other sets of neighbors and a host of mice and cockroaches. All our bathrooms had windows that vented into a central air shaft in the middle of the building, so we heard a good bit of everything that went on in our neighbors' lives. It's hard to hide things in such a setting: daily habits, music preferences, familial fights, alcohol problems—and the list goes on. It's hard not to get to know your neighbors or to pretend the homeless folks and prostitutes down at the corner do not exist.

The raw realities of life were much more visible in our part of the city than anywhere I had lived before. And surprisingly, I have been grateful for this. It is not that I like all the messiness, pain and suffering we saw. Not at all. But I do like that we actually saw and acknowledged the brokenness and need instead of hiding it or pretending it did not exist. I'm grateful for having fewer barriers, fewer pretenses and more honest interactions with people of incredibly diverse backgrounds and outlooks.

One of the biggest lessons I learned from this move is that we don't realize just how insulated we are from life until we are actually faced with reality. I used to complain about being too sheltered, but the truth is that I found the stability comforting. Voluntarily moving out of my safety zone and giving up some of that shelter was not easy. It became especially challenging when our car was broken into and when one of my roommates was mugged at gunpoint just outside our building.

Stepping out to face reality can be tough, but until we do so, it will be hard to clearly see, hear and feel what is going on. It will be even harder to know what we need to do and how we can help. When we come out of denial and bring the problems out into the open, however, we are in much better shape to understand and address them.

The Underlying Problem of Insulation

It's the same thing with this planet.

It's astonishing just how little many of us, especially in my generation, know about what it takes to sustain our everyday demands—and how hard it can be to find these things out. The vast majority of us don't know where our food or clothes come from and how they get to us ("the store" isn't a good answer). We don't know where we get our power from, only that it is always on hand. At the end of the day, when we put that big bag of garbage out for pickup, that is the last we ever think of it. But where does all our trash and wastewater go?

If we had a better grasp on reality and a fuller picture of the impacts of our current lifestyles, however, we would be more challenged to change and more knowledgeable about how to go about it.

The previous chapter looked at the parable of the prodigal son as analogous to our situation today: as a society, and often as a church, we have largely wandered away from God and splurged his creation frivolously on ourselves, to the point where we now face environmental crises around the globe.

As in the parable, coming back "home" to God and to his purposes starts with, but does not culminate in, a *decision* to return. This decision, while extremely important, is for us only the beginning of a lifelong process of re-visioning what it means to live for Christ in a wayward society. In one sense, we are immediately welcomed as full members into the family of God. In another sense, however, we are only beginning to discern and internalize what it means to be part of this great family.

This growing process can be challenging. In many ways, the world tempts us to pursue blissfully ignorant lives of comfort, safety and security for ourselves. There is very little in what Jesus teaches or models that affirms these goals, however. Instead, we are more often called to lives of intentional community, meaningful service and joyful sacrifice for Christ and for our neighbors. This has implications for all aspects of our lives.

As a result, we need to discern attentively what the gospel calls us to today and then be lovingly intentional about living it out. It will take time and concerted effort to get from who we are and how we are living now to who God created us to be and how he calls us to live in his society. This includes relearning what it means to be good children, good neighbors and good stewards.

Such growth may not be natural for us, but the first step is to remove the layers of surrounding insulation that hide us from reality.

A Case in Point

I always heard that saving power is good, but I used to be lazy about turning lights off, shutting appliances down, changing light bulbs to energy-efficient models and the like. Then I learned that about half of our electricity in the United States comes from coal and that it is one of the dirtiest ways to generate electricity.[2]

Coal-fired power plants are currently the largest polluter of toxic mercury—a heavy metal that has serious effects on human and ecosystem health. In 2006 the U.S. government issued 3,080 warnings against eating game fish from many lakes and rivers due to mercury poisoning.[3]

Aside from the mercury, these coal plants are also major emitters of sixty-seven other air toxins, nitrous oxides, sulfur dioxide, carbon dioxide and soot.[4] This pollution exacerbates respiratory diseases, especially among those lower-income populations that live around the power plants, and is responsible for causing up to 24,000 premature deaths in the United States each year from heart disease, asthma and lung cancer.[5] And all of this does not include damage caused as a result of mining and refining coal.

There are multiple ways to mine coal, but mountaintop removal mining (MTR) is perhaps the most unsustainable. MTR is a growing form of coal mining being used daily in Appalachian states such as Tennessee, Kentucky and West Virginia. It involves blowing the tops off mountains to reach seams of coal hidden inside. At the time of writing, an estimated three million pounds of explosives are used to take down mountains every day in West Virginia alone.[6]

It may sound ridiculous, but coal companies adopt this technique because it is a lot cheaper and faster to blast away the earth with dynamite than to pay miners to tunnel through it. It makes good sense if you are in it for short-term monetary profits. The blasted earth is then bulldozed into adjacent valleys and slurry—the toxic waste left over from washing the coal—sits in huge reservoirs nearby.

There are many problems with MTR mining. First, it is a serious degradation of the creation we were entrusted to be good stewards over. Entire mountains are destroyed, forests turned to wasteland and streams contaminated with heavy metals. But on top of its effects on the earth,

MTR mining devastates local communities. The groundwater in many locations is now undrinkable, the air is filled with asthma-causing coal dust, flying debris litters yards, human health is compromised, and extreme floods resulting from deforestation have resulted in many deaths and millions of dollars in damage. Local communities have joined together through grassroots organizations such as the Ohio Valley Environmental Coalition, Coal River Mountain Watch, Mountain Justice Summer and Christians for the Mountains to take a stand, but they struggle to compete against the deep pockets of the coal industry and their politicians.

There is legislation on the books, such as the federal Clean Water Act of 1972, to help ensure that mining is not done in an overly harmful way. Sadly, enforcement is weak and industry executives are rich enough that they do not have to live with the environmental, social and health consequences of their own mining operations.

I was shocked to find out that this injustice is still going on, right

Mountaintop removal near Kayford Mountain in West Virginia. Photo by Vivian Stockman.

Dispatch: Allen Johnson, Christians for the Mountains

The Appalachian War Zone

Real-world global economics can be summed up in the following story: A couple of years ago Larry Gibson was in New York as a member of a panel discussing energy policy. For twenty years Gibson has wept as his beloved ancestral surroundings of lovely, lush mountains and running brooks morph into surreal moonscapes of haunting desolation.

During the discussion, one of the panelists, a Protestant minister, explained the facts of life, "energy speaking," to Gibson. His words went like this: "Larry, I'm sure it's tough for you to see the mountains and forests you grew up with drastically changed," he said. "But you need to know there are only a few people living in your neighborhood, while there are millions of folks in the rest of our nation who need the energy contained in your mountains. We must have energy in order to exist as a strong nation. You therefore have a duty to sacrifice your own personal interests for the good of the rest of the country."

I remember well the first time I led a group of Christians to Gibson's Kayford Mountain property, precariously perched as an island amid a massive sea of ruined mountaintop. As host, Gibson was trying to remain civil, yet he was visibly edgy with us Christians present. "That preacher wanted me to sacrifice my homeland so everyone else can have cheap electricity and live comfortable lives. What about my life? What about my neighbors? Why, we don't matter; we're all just dumb hillbillies to him. I guess that's what people think about our homeland, a 'national energy sacrifice zone.'"

In Gibson's experience, the churches had been of no

use. "Where have you been?" he railed. "Our mountains are being destroyed, our lives ruined, our culture annihilated, and the churches are nowhere to be found. The coal company helps build a picnic shelter for a church or someone in the church drives a coal truck, so the church says nothing."

Mountaintop removal is just one more travesty of justice and exploitation that trails back millennia. The biblical prophets railed against economies that brought riches and comfort to some through oppression and exploitation of others. One only needs to travel through the Appalachian coalfields to see abject poverty, community desolation and environmental destruction, the dregs of an extraordinary wealth carted to mansions and boardrooms in faraway states.

We as Christians can wring our sympathetic hands at injustice and then go on pursuing our comfortable lives. Talk is cheap. Or we can do something. Begin a journey of acting out our faith. Like, when we aren't using the room lights, for Christ's sake, turn 'em off!

under our noses. It was also sobering to realize that most of the coal extracted from Appalachia goes to generate electricity that we consume in the rest of the nation.

Not long after learning all this, I made it down to Appalachia to see if MTR mining really is as bad as it sounds. The photos and video I had seen leading up to my visit could not fully prepare me for the extent of the tragedy.

Down in West Virginia, I was warmly received by Larry Gibson on Kayford Mountain and Allen Johnson with Christians for the Mountains. Standing at the edge of Larry's property at the top of Kayford, I looked out as far as I could see onto a silent and eerily decimated moonscape that used to be lush and diverse forest. I thought of the hymn that begins "I sing the mighty power of God that made the mountains rise" and watched as men in mammoth-sized dump trucks carted one of God's mountains away piece by piece. I thought of the hymn "This Is My Father's World" and burned with indignation at the injustice being heaped on God's land and his people.

My trip down to the mountains of West Virginia had a deep impact on me, as it does for many who see what is going on down there. I witnessed firsthand the effects of our increasing energy consumption, and now I am much more careful about how I use energy. I no longer feel it is a chore to switch off the lights or hang my clothes on a line instead of using an electric dryer. Instead, I find myself far more grateful for the electricity I use and eager to find ways to use less.

Before learning about coal-generated electricity, I was okay with being ignorant because it meant I didn't feel responsible for anything bad that was happening. Ignorance is not a good excuse, however, and we can do a better job of facing reality together. Only then will we have the knowledge and impulse to make the right changes.

As William Wilberforce, the great British abolitionist and outspoken evangelical Christian, put it when exposing the cruelties of the slave trade: "Having heard all this you may choose to look the other way . . . but you can never say again that you did not know."[7] Looking away, however, is not a good option: "Anyone, then, who knows the good he ought to do and doesn't do it, sins" (Jas 4:17).

My perspectives changed once I stepped out and actually saw more of what was going on to generate electricity. The reality I uncovered began to have implications for the lifestyle I was living.

Synthetic Reality

A modern challenge to our ability to live in reality lies in our growing dependence on some forms of technology—the virtual world in particular. Now that we can do almost everything on a computer or online—shopping, working, banking, listening to sermons, playing games and catching up with friends—increasingly more of life is lived in front of a screen.

There are benefits to this age of advanced technology and the Internet. Communication is many times faster now than in the days of snail mail, and we have access to exponentially more knowledge, tools and resources at our fingertips. It can even be good for the environment. Shopping online is one such example; it can use less fossil fuel by saving trips to the store, and it is easier to buy and sell used products (thereby saving money and virgin resources).

But these benefits are balanced out by the potential harms. Besides wearing out our eyesight faster, the more we live online or in front of a monitor means the less life we live in person. My generation and those to follow are coming of age in an increasingly technologically connected yet relationally isolated world; we may have literally hundreds of friends on Facebook and yet feel lonely because we don't get to interact with most of them in real life.

Part of the trouble is that this sort of virtual community is not as real as it claims to be. Instead, it can become a way to temporarily escape from the real world by creating or investing in an alternate reality. In doing so, we put off having to deal with our real problems because they no longer seem to exist.

For instance, in real life I may be struggling to pass chemistry class, but on the computer I'm a highly skilled mercenary hunting down and killing terrorists. In real life I may be a recent college graduate without a job, but on Second Life I'm a successful young lawyer. In real life I may be self-conscious about gaining weight, but on MySpace I need only to post photos that make me look slim.

While I'm not suggesting that it is wrong to make use of the Internet or to take regular breaks from the daily grind and occasionally step back from our problems and insecurities, we should not consistently hide from these things either. The risk is that the more we get sucked into virtual worlds, the less connected we stay to the real world; the more we stare into a screen, the less we see what is actually going on around us.

Such technology has great potential to connect us to each other and to what is going on in the world. It also, however, has the power to further insulate us from reality.

The Model of Incarnational Living

So how can we overcome our insulation and engage more directly with reality when it comes to the environment—or other issues, for that matter? Jesus had something to say about this. In the parable of the good Samaritan (see Lk 10:30-37), he teaches us what it means to be a good neighbor.

The story goes like this: A Jew was walking on a dangerous road and got mugged by bandits and left half dead on the roadside. Both a priest and a scribe came along and quickly moved on their way without so much as lifting a finger for their countryman.

When a Samaritan came onto the scene, however, he showed great compassion for someone who should have been his enemy (Jews and Samaritans didn't get along). He took notice long enough to grasp the situation and then was moved to compassion. He got down from his donkey to care for his wounded neighbor, inconveniencing himself and putting his own life at risk. Expending personal resources, he not only washed and bandaged the man, but even took him to the nearest inn and paid for his entire recovery.

It wasn't enough for the Samaritan to tell the next Roman soldier he saw about the mugging or to hand down some coins or clothes in pity. Instead, he stepped out of his comfort zone, got his hands dirty and sacrificed his own resources to show love and bring healing. Jesus ends the parable by calling his listeners to be such neighbors—to go and do likewise.

More than what Jesus had to say, however, is the compelling model he lived out. He is the ultimate good Samaritan. He saw us in freefall and stooped down through eternity to pick us up. His name Emmanuel means "God with us," and the Gospel of John begins with the astonishing statement that "the Word [Jesus Christ] became flesh and made his dwelling among us" (Jn 1:14).

This model is one of incarnation—Christ willingly became a person and walked among us. He lived on this same earth, breathed the same air and drank the same water. He participated as a fully embodied member of this global ecosystem and, in doing so, also affirmed the goodness of creation.

In the same way that God sent his Son into the world, so Christ sends us into the world. The apostle Paul makes this clear when writing to the church in Philippi:

> Your attitude should be the same as that of Christ Jesus: Who, being in very nature God, did not consider equality with God something to be grasped, but made himself nothing, taking the very nature of a servant, being made in human likeness. And being found in appearance as a man, he humbled himself and became obedient to death—even death on a cross! Therefore God exalted him to the highest place and gave him the name that is above every name, that at the name of Jesus every knee should bow, in heaven and on earth and under the earth, and every tongue confess that Jesus Christ is Lord, to the glory of God the Father. (Phil 2:5-11)

The model we have been given is not one of reaching down but of incarnating among and fellowshiping with one another. We are called to break through boundaries of separation and to serve from within the place of need. This is true when we think of serving the poor and oppressed who are affected by environmental degradation, and it is true when we think about our relationship to the nonhuman creation.

God intends us to know intimately and to relate to each other and the rest of his creation: the first task for the human pair was to name all the creatures in the Garden of Eden. How many of the species left in our own backyard can we identify today? When we read the Gospels, it is clear from his teachings that Christ was well acquainted with the society and ecosystem around him. We were given his image to be just and compassionate rulers of the world, but how can we fulfill this calling unless we try to understand and connect with one another and the rest of creation?

Experiments in Incarnational Earthcare

We more authentically experience God's original intentions for the world when we participate in the good work of tending his creation, whatever form that takes for each of us. This is the underlying premise of A Rocha.

A Rocha (AR) is an organization of Christians in conservation that is actively working in over twenty countries on five continents. It was started in 1983 by Peter and Miranda Harris, an Anglican missionary couple who moved from England to southern Portugal, where they established a field studies center to help the local community protect a valuable estuary from outside development.

Since then, A Rocha projects have sprung up in Kenya, Ghana, Lebanon, India, France, the Czech Republic, Brazil, the United Kingdom, Canada, the United States and elsewhere. These various national projects are all very different because they reflect the local culture and needs. What they all share, however, is an emphasis on moving past discussing creation care to fully living it out within Christian community.

For instance, AR Kenya runs an ecotourism project with communities in the coastal district of Malindi, helping them protect what little remains of the once extensive Arabuko-Sokoke Forest, while generating enough income to send their children to secondary school. AR India works alongside the Indian government and communities to understand and minimize human-elephant conflicts in an effort that both saves human lives and property and conserves highly threatened Asian elephant populations.

In the United States, AR partnered with Asbury College in the summer of 2007 to coordinate recycling at Ichthus, an annual outdoor Christian music festival in Wilmore, Kentucky. For several days, between 15,000 and 20,000 people from all over the country stream onto a grassy field under the blazing summer sun to hear their favorite Christian bands play. This many people go through a lot of plastic beverage bottles and aluminum cans, but there had never been much of a recycling program. Everything had ended up at the landfill. So, following up on a last-minute lead and with lots of help from Andy Bathje and his hardworking Asbury students, our AR USA team scrambled together a bunch of recycling bins and organized a collection plan.

Since people were not used to recycling at Ichthus, this plan involved not only emptying the recycling bins, but also rummaging through the regular trash bins to remove the numerous plastic bottles from sticky

Students from A Rocha Wheaton testing water quality as part of an amphibian biodiversity project in the local forest preserves. Photo by Ben Lowe.

piles of old chewing gum, soggy funnel cakes and half-eaten burgers. It was a sweaty, smelly, exhausting and humbling affair. We did it for free because we had to, but we did it cheerfully because we were doing it for Christ.

Over time the crowds started catching on and throwing their bottles in the right bins. Some folks even grabbed empty bags and helped us. In the end, we were able to retrieve and deliver approximately 78,000 bottles to a very surprised local recycling facility.

Whether through recycling at Ichthus or in other diverse projects around the globe, AR provides a down-to-earth vision of what it looks like when Christians get up from the pews and come together on the ground to care for God's creation. Many AR staff and supporters are not vocational scientists (though some certainly are, and the organization is well known for its solid science) but are drawn by the opportunity to come alongside their neighbors, roll up their sleeves, and get their hands dirty making a difference for Christ and his creation.

Making the Move

Based on Christ's model, the parable of the good Samaritan and the experiences of A Rocha, here are three practical principles in moving from being insulated from much of the world to engaging it incarnationally. How these actually look naturally varies from person to person and group to group.

Step out humbly. Step out of isolation and get down to earth. Explore our surroundings—both human and nonhuman—and find out what is really going on and what is needed.

In general, stepping out could mean getting outdoors more intentionally, talking to longtime community members at church and checking out the various active local organizations or ministries. Good questions to ask include "What natural resources do we use?" "Where do they come from?" and "What are the social and environmental impacts of our lifestyle?"

Many towns and cities have their own websites with information on local energy sources, waste policies and other environmental issues. We do not engage as experts with answers but as servants eager to learn, in need of grace and considering others better than ourselves (see Phil 2:3).

Build intentional community. How can we love our neighbors if we don't know who they are, how we are affecting them and what their needs are? This is why A Rocha places great emphasis on being a relational organization in which we experience life together and work within and across our respective cultures. We certainly need to build community with those immediately around us (by plugging into our neighborhoods, schools and churches) but, in such a global society, there is also no excuse for not reaching out to and connecting with brothers and sisters around the world. We are called to share in their suffering, just as we are called to share in the suffering of Christ (see 1 Cor 12:26; Phil 3:10; 1 Pet 4:13).

To this end, there are some signs that an interesting idea known as eco-twinning may be gaining traction through the All Africa Conference of Churches and the Alliance of Religions and Conservation. Twinning is an established practice by some denominations and international ministries of linking two churches together from completely different geographical areas. Eco-twinning involves pairing churches in the Global North with churches in the Global South in communities that are suffering because of environmental degradation. These sister churches then have the opportunity to develop intentional long-term relationships that include visiting one another, sharing resources and partnering together to address environmental injustices.

Practice sacrificial love. Faith, if action does not go along with it, is dead (see Jas 2:17). We must take the biblical principles of neighbor love and stewardship and apply them to address the problems we find around us. Sacrificial love takes countless forms, depending on the specific context and need. Volunteering hours on end to sort through recyclables at Ichthus is one example. Drying laundry on a clothesline to save energy is another act of sacrificial love directed toward God, his creation and our neighbors in Appalachia, where some of the fuel for our electricity comes from.

Worth the Cost

True creation stewardship—stepping out humbly, building intentional community, practicing sacrificial love—demands a lot from us.

This is not a popular message in a world that worships easy fixes. We want to believe that new technology—not conservation—is the key to solving environmental problems. Some people hold that we can pollute as much as we want as long as we pay for carbon offsets elsewhere. We often balk at the idea of sacrifice, yet sacrifice is exactly what's needed.

This call to follow Christ, love our neighbor and care for the planet will exact a toll. It will cost our conscience. It will cost some of our space. It will cost some of our comfort. It will cost some of our time and even our money.

But these costs pale in comparison to the importance of our message: we are talking about an integral part of the gospel here—the good news of the kingdom of God and all it entails. And the costs pale in comparison to the value of our stewardship: we are partnering with Christ to bring about the reconciliation of all things back to God and to his shalom. Christ willingly sacrificed his life by dying on the cross to fulfill this same mission. What price is too high for us to pay?

This sounds extreme, and it is.

It can be very easy to be radical, sacrificial or subversive for its own sake or to achieve a sense of self-righteousness. But if we really believe that God calls us to love our neighbors and to be stewards of his creation, and if we really believe that the greedy exploitation of people and natural resources is wrong and sinful, then our mission is clear: we must fully engage in all aspects of loving our neighbors and caring for creation with everything God has given us.

And we can joyfully persevere in the journey from insulation to incarnation and from safety to sacrifice, rejoicing in the ultimate reality that every step closer to God and his kingdom is supremely worth the effort.

Uplink: Peter Harris, Founder, A Rocha

It shouldn't surprise us that a straightforward Christian concern for creation should lead us to making the connections that we find Ben making in this chapter. Anyone who looks with clear eyes at places such as the Appalachian mountains can only grieve if they believe the mountains are not simply "natural resources" that we need for a lifestyle of excessive consumption, but are a created reality, made lovingly by the Lord of everything we see. Neither can Christian eyes rest only on ravaged landscapes if they understand that the people who live within them are known and loved by their creator God. Toxic run-off and social destruction are also within our appalled and grieving gaze if we make the journey as Ben has done. The stories of the people and their broken communities will also take their place in our hearts before long.

If we, like Ben, go beyond our insulation and follow the paths of Christ, which always lead outside the comfortable walls, we will soon see more clearly where we too fit into the picture. Neither will it be long before we discover that it will never be our words that give our truest response to the challenges we encounter. It is not what we say that will connect us to the story of mountaintop removal or urban deprivation, but a true relationship with our Creator.

That will then guide how we choose to live with what we have come to understand and see through his eyes. Then how we use God's creation in our daily lives, how we power our existence, what we use, what we eat, all become questions about faith. The choices of how to clean our clothes, how to get around our cities, how to live in the times and places we find ourselves, begin to take its rightful place in the dialogue of Christians with their God, and the incarnation starts to look earthy indeed. Paul spelled it out for us when he preached in Athens that God "determined the times set for them and the exact places where they should live . . . so that men would seek him and perhaps reach out for him and find him" (Acts 17:26-27). God has been encouraging us all to find him more profoundly and to begin to live like Christians.

Part 2

Changing Our Communities

4

The Heat Is On
The Current Creation Care Movement and the Climate Crisis That Sparked It

Christian people should surely have been in the vanguard of the movement for environmental responsibility, because of our doctrines of creation and stewardship. Did God make the world? Does he sustain it? Has he committed its resources to our care? His personal concern for his own creation should be sufficient to inspire us to be equally concerned.

John R. W. Stott

Is it getting hot in here, or is it just me? The icecaps may be melting, but so is the church's frozen stance toward caring for the planet. The global-warming crisis has become the alarm to reawaken Christians to our moral responsibility to steward God's creation.

What was once barely a trickle of concern is now surging into a flood of action to protect the earth. Prominent pastors like Rick Warren and Joel Hunter, along with influential ministries such as World Vision and *Christianity Today,* are becoming increasingly vocal about the need to take creation care seriously.

Christian colleges have started teaching about environmental stewardship through chapel messages, new courses and other special programming, while parachurch ministries on secular campuses (such as InterVarsity Christian Fellowship) are inviting guest speakers for creation care talks and engaging in positive interactions with existing environmental groups on their campuses. Shorter College, a Southern Baptist–affiliated institution in Georgia with about three thousand students, went so far as to designate environmentalism as the student theme for the 2008-2009 academic year, which means, among other things, that the students will be given reading assignments on creation care.

Meanwhile, churches of all demographics and denominations are devoting sermons and teaching series to this issue. Rob Bell and Matt Krick at Mars Hill Bible Church (Grandville, Michigan) organized a five-week series titled "God Is Green" in 2007. Bill Hybels preached a creation care message at Willow Creek Community Church (South Barrington, Illinois) in early 2008, during which he declared that the congregation would continue to hear more about this issue in the church.

The Chinese Bible Church of Greater Boston (Lexington, Massachusetts)—one of the larger and more prominent Chinese churches in the United States—has addressed creation care issues in multiple sermons and is working through its social concerns committee to identify ways that the church can continue raising awareness and improving its environmental impact.

River City Community Church—a young and intentionally multicultural congregation in the Humboldt Park neighborhood of inner-city Chicago—held a creation care service in 2008, during which everyone in the congregation was given a free, energy-efficient compact fluorescent light bulb.

The above examples just barely scratch the surface of the awakening that is sweeping through much of the church. From 2006 to 2008, Matthew Sleeth, author of *Serve God, Save the Planet,* spoke in more than a hundred churches and on thirty college campuses, with new invitations coming in continuously.

More and more of the church is finally starting to think and talk about the importance of creation care. Beyond talk, however, countless Christians in the pews are responding to these sermons and to their own concerns by making practical changes in their lifestyles and communities. It used to be that when I told people I was studying environmental science, they usually smiled politely and moved on to other topics. Now, however, people appear increasingly excited that I work for a Christian conservation organization and are eager to share what they are doing to make a difference in their homes, schools and workplaces.

The church and the climate have something important in common these days: they are both changing faster than expected.

A Changing Climate

This book is not specifically about global warming. Because it is one of the top issues of the day, however, it is worth focusing on the basic discussion around climate change and how Christians are responding to this specific threat.

Eleven of the twelve hottest years in recorded history (up until 2008) have occurred since 1995.[1] In the summer of 2003, a heat wave that hit Europe caused 35,000 deaths and was statistically attributed to the effects of a warming climate.[2] Glaciers and ice sheets are also on an overall retreat, and sea levels have been rising at a rate of three millimeters per year since 1993.[3] Meanwhile, atmospheric concentrations of greenhouse gases such as carbon dioxide, methane and nitrous oxide have skyrocketed since the beginning of the twentieth century due mainly to accelerated deforestation, increased travel and the Industrial Revolution. Are these changing climate patterns and increasing concentrations of greenhouse gases just a freaky coincidence? Most scientists no longer think so.

Global warming—more accurately called global climate change—refers to long-term changes in the average climate of the entire planet. Basically, data collected by scientists around the globe show that climate patterns are changing unnaturally quickly and the earth is getting warmer overall. This does not mean that some places will not get colder. It does mean, however, that if you took the temperatures for every spot on earth and averaged them throughout the year for multiple years, you would see this average rising.

Heat from the sun is the energy source that ultimately drives our weather (volcanic activity impacts weather as well, but on a smaller scale and less consistently). Based on this principle, a warmer climate will result in different weather patterns and more extreme events, such as droughts, floods, heat waves and cold spells. It may help give rise to stronger storms and hurricanes, although the current models may not have enough resolution to conclusively demonstrate this. Also, as many of the glaciers and ice sheets continue to melt and as the oceans get warmer and expand, sea levels will continue to rise. Having grown up on the low-lying island of Singapore, I do not need to be reminded what will happen if the sea level rises much further. Small islands and coastal regions around the world—home to major cities and huge populations of people—may eventually be submerged.

In the United States, the impacts of what the Bush Administration affirms as "man-made global warming" include increased deaths from heat and climate-worsened smog, worsening water shortages, longer and more intense wildfire seasons, expanding insect infestations and pest outbreaks, and more.[4]

So, depending on how far all this goes, global warming is a problem. A big problem. In response to early concerns, the United Nations Environment Programme and World Meteorological Organization came together in 1988 to commission the Intergovernmental Panel on Climate Change (IPCC). The IPCC gathered thousands of scientists from countries all around the world to analyze the latest climate research and synthesize findings into authoritative assessments, which have been released in 1990, 1995, 2001 and 2007.

At first there was a good deal of uncertainty in the findings and predictions of the IPCC, but each assessment has become more conclusive than the last. Some questions still exist, however, and can be organized into three main questions:

What is the cause? The international science community has joined in agreement that increasing greenhouse gases are a major cause of climate change. Greenhouse gases act as a blanket on the earth, holding in heat from the sun. As more greenhouse gases collect in the atmosphere, the blanket grows thicker and the earth gets warmer.[5] Through burning fossil fuels such as oil, cutting down forests and a myriad of other activities, humans are currently adding millions of tons of greenhouse gases to the atmosphere. Greenhouse gases are also released through natural processes such as volcanic eruptions. Even so, the definitive 2007 IPCC assessment report gave a conservative 90-percent probability estimate that humans are responsible for causing the climate to change.[6] Another potential cause for warming is variations in the amount of heat the sun gives off (especially through bursts of energy called solar flares), but this is no longer considered an important factor in the current warming trend.

How bad will it get? A range of estimates is given based on results obtained from multiple models and scenarios. The average global surface temperature has already risen by about 0.75 degrees Celsius in the last century. The same IPCC report as above predicted a probable additional increase in average temperatures from 1.8 to 4.0 degrees Celsius, an average sea level rise of between 28 and 43 centimeters and the disappearance of arctic summer sea ice sometime after 2050. These numbers may sound small, but they are only averages (highs and lows in various locations will be much greater), and our planet functions in a delicate balance; it does not take much change to result in large impacts. For instance, when one thousand feet of solid ice sat on top of the city of Chicago during the last ice age, the global average temperature was only about 4 degrees Celsius cooler than today.[7] The exact impacts of the current warming depend on how much we manage to prepare and adapt in time, but it is already expected to result in millions of additional environmental refugees, increased deaths from extreme weather (such as in the 2003 European heat wave) and a host of other serious consequences. Ecosystems will also struggle to adapt in time, and the more vulnerable species will go extinct.

What should be done about it? This is where the greatest amount of debate exists. There are two major extremes and a whole range of combined approaches in-between. One approach is to focus efforts on drastically reducing our greenhouse gas emissions to slow down global warming. This can be done through carbon cap and trade programs, carbon offsetting and international agreements. Another approach proposes that reducing emissions is not cost-effective, so we should invest available resources in adapting to the impacts of climate change instead of trying to stop them. Responses would include building dikes to hold back seawater and helping coastal communities relocate further inland. Both approaches have strengths and weaknesses, and the best solution is likely a combination of the two. Regardless of the specific approach, however, it is clear that we need to be doing something.

Sorting Through the Evidence

There is no such thing as a complete consensus in today's world. There will always be debate over whether something is true or not. The challenge for each of us, therefore, is to carefully consider the data, compare it with relevant personal experience and trusted testimonies and then make an informed decision.

For a while, I straddled the fence on whether I thought global warming was real. My science textbooks told me it was, but what I was hearing in church told me it was not. This was confusing, and for a while I just ignored the issue altogether. But the more I got involved in creation care efforts and the more peers invited me to get involved in climate projects, the more friends asked me questions about the science.[8]

Soon it became the proverbial elephant in the room, and I realized I would have to look at the evidence more closely and try to make a decision. This came to a head during my junior year, when Ryan Hobert at the United Nations Foundation invited me to participate in a strategy session on campus climate issues with other student organizers from around the country. I accepted the invitation with the realization that it was time for me to get off the fence. It took me about six months of serious consideration before I felt assured enough to take a position. Here is how I went about it:

First, I tried to push past the polarizing rhetoric and consider the data. Climate change starts as a scientific issue, and the most authoritative science seems to consistently agree that the earth is warming, that human actions are a significant cause, that the effects will be largely negative and that we know how to reduce it.

Second, I compared it with my own relevant experiences. One particular experience has played a large role in this process: fisheries research on the shores of Lake Tanganyika in Tanzania in 2006. Lake Tanganyika is the second deepest in the world and holds just over 10 percent of all available freshwater at any one time. It is also home to a wealth of amazing fish and invertebrate species found nowhere else in the world—an awesome showcase of God's creativity and majesty. These fish form a vibrant fishery that local communities have long relied on for food.

Recently, however, parts of this critical fishery have started crashing. Fishermen are now catching fewer and smaller fish, even though they continue to fish as they have for generations. People are growing very concerned. These villages are some of the poorest in the world and have few alternatives if the fish run out. At the end of the twentieth century, scientists found that an increase in average temperatures in the region was causing a decrease in biological productivity in the lake. This meant that the fish had less food and so their populations also started to shrink.

Basically, then, a warming in the region (corresponding to the average warming around the globe for that same period) was likely responsible for the shrinking fishery.[9] The scientists published the data in a prestigious scientific journal, but then what? While I was in Tanzania, I could try to explain the problem to confused fishermen, but I had no solution to offer. After all, it was not their fault the climate was warming—and they are not the ones with two or more cars in each driveway.

It is sad that they end up being the ones to bear the cost. Seeing firsthand this example of how global warming is already affecting some of the world's poorest people—the least of these—has had a profound effect on my life.

In sorting through all the climate-change hype and confusion, I also turned to people I trust who know more about the issue than I do. As a Christian, this was easy: there are some top-notch climate scientists who are devout Christians. One notable example is Sir John Houghton, arguably the world's leading climate expert and a very articulate Christian, who speaks openly about how he integrates science with his faith. Throughout his long and distinguished career, he has served as a physics professor at Oxford University, chief executive of the United Kingdom Meteorological Office and chairman of scientific assessment (Working Group 1) for the IPCC from 1988 to 2001. When he says something about the climate, it carries serious weight in both the science and the faith communities.

In addition to Sir John, I also had a very helpful conversation with Dean Ohlman, a senior leader in the creation care movement. Dean is

Dispatch: Sir John Speaks

By 2001, we were able to say much more clearly that it was very likely that the warming we had seen since the 1970s was largely due to human activity. And since 2001, the science community has become much more concerned, because the evidence seems to be becoming much stronger.

People who are likely to be most disadvantaged because of climate change live in poorer countries. They haven't the infrastructure to cope with the problems of sea-level rise, floods and droughts. Indeed, the incidence of such events will tend to be stronger in subtropical areas—southern Asia, South America and the Caribbean—than in the industrialized world of mid-latitudes.

If Christians around the world really got behind action on issues of this kind, we could very strongly address the need to protect the poor and provide for them. And that could make an enormous difference.[a]

---

[a]Excerpts from David Neff, "Looking After Creation" (an interview with Sir John Houghton), *Christianity Today,* April 2006 <http://www.christianity today.com/ct/2006/004/16.77.html>.

very good at communicating complicated concepts clearly, so I asked him for advice on reaching a decision about climate change. Our conversation went something like this:

"Think about having a stomach ache that becomes so uncomfortable you go in to see a doctor," Dean said. "The doctor runs some tests and tells you it looks like cancer, but, hey, you should get a second opinion just in case. Being a cautious person, you actually go to one hundred doctors for diagnosis. Of them, ninety think you have stomach cancer and need to be operated on immediately. The remaining ten suggest it may simply be a bad case of indigestion. They want to see how it develops and ask you to come back for more tests next month if it doesn't go away.

"So, Ben," Dean continued, "which set of advice will you listen to?"

I started to see where this was going. "Well, I would want to believe the ten that think it may be indigestion," I replied, "but I would almost certainly act on the advice of the ninety who recommend an operation."

Dean's simple analogy hits home. The majority of experts have reached a strong consensus that human-induced climate change is real and that it is no longer worth the risk to "wait and see" what happens. We are already committed to a certain level of warming, they warn, but if we dawdle longer, it may be too late to avoid grave damage.

At the end of the day, I considered all the information I had about climate change, and then I prayed about it. The decision weighed heavily on my heart for some time, as my close friends know well. But in the end it was time to settle on where I would stand and, by agreeing we had enough certainty that climate change was real and urgent, I also committed myself to trying to do something about it. After all, if we believe something is true, how we live should reflect that belief.

Compared to many of my peers, I was slow to reach these conclusions on global warming. And, in reality, sustaining this position is an ongoing process of evaluation, as more information becomes available and new insights come to light. As with many issues in life, this one is not always straightforward. It is reassuring, then, that God does not expect us to be all-knowing; he simply expects us to be faithful stewards.

Stewardship can be defined as making good decisions for the future, based on the best information we have at the present. Most of us are not climate scientists. If the best information available now points to a warming planet, our responsibility is to address it. Even if the scientists are mistaken and we later find that climate change is not a problem (a highly unlikely scenario), we still did the right thing by taking action on their earlier warnings. God does not expect us to act on what we have no way of knowing; he does, however, hold us accountable for what we do know and yet do not take to heart. We should always try to understand the science behind these issues better, but we should not let our pursuit of further knowledge distract us from taking the right steps now.

This is especially the case because the steps being proposed now, such as reducing pollution, saving energy, cutting back on our dependency on oil and more, would all be good things to do even if global warming were not happening.

A Changing Church

It is not just about the science, however. Global warming is also a moral issue, and this is why it is so important for Christians to take a stand. On one hand, if we choose poorly or simply hold off making any decisions on this, we will be held all the more accountable by God for the damage we contributed against the earth and our neighbors. On the other hand, if we choose well, God will rejoice in our faithfulness as we better reflect his intentions and qualities to the rest of creation.

For many years, however, the evangelical church has remained largely disengaged from environmental issues in general and climate change in particular; we have committed sins of omission when it comes to environmental stewardship. One notable exception was the Evangelical Declaration on the Care of Creation, first released in 1994 and endorsed by hundreds of prominent church leaders around the world.[10]

Aside from that extraordinary push, crucial issues such as abortion, prayer in schools, homosexuality and evolution became our main targets. We debated vigorously that God created the earth, but then we forgot to take care of it as he asked. We focused on these few "priority issues" so much that they became the only issues we seemed to care about. There were always vocal minorities that tried to attract attention to other causes like AIDS and the environment. For the most part, however, they remained just that—vocal minorities—and had little effect on the church's position as a whole.

This all began to change at the start of the new millennium. In particular, the issue of global warming started getting too big to ignore. Climate change was receiving more attention in the press and, at the same time, Christians started hearing more from some surprising sources—other Christians.

A big mover on global warming is the Reverend Dr. Jim Ball, executive director of the Evangelical Environmental Network. At the end of 2002,

Ball launched the almost-legendary What Would Jesus Drive? campaign.[11] In an effort to highlight transportation pollution and promote a better driving ethic among Christians, he and his wife drove a hybrid car from Texas to Washington, D.C., stopping along the way to speak to churches, politicians and the press. The tour was an inspiring success and was featured in more than four thousand media stories within only six months.

Earlier in the same year, the John Ray Initiative in the United Kingdom and the Au Sable Institute of Environmental Studies in the United States cosponsored Climate Forum 2002 in Oxford, England, to address the issue of human-induced global warming. The conference resulted in the Oxford Declaration on Global Warming and marked the first time Christian scientists, policymakers and church leaders worked together to address the church's role in the climate-change problem.[12]

As a follow-up to that forum, in 2004 leaders at the National Association of Evangelicals (NAE), Christianity Today and the Evangelical Environmental Network organized a gathering of key evangelicals in the United States, who wrote the Sandy Cove Covenant on creation care.[13]

In 2004, the NAE also launched their Re:Vision campaign with a statement titled "For the Health of the Nation: An Evangelical Call to Civic Responsibility."[14] In it they list seven principles that Christians should focus action on, including creation care.

Then, in January 2006, Ball led more than one hundred evangelical leaders in signing the Evangelical Climate Initiative (ECI), the most emphatic Christian statement to date, calling for active government action to reduce global carbon emissions and other activities that contribute to global warming. Signatories to the ECI now include prominent pastors like Rick Warren, Joel Hunter, Bill Hybels, Leith Anderson, Rob Bell and the presidents of more than thirty-five leading evangelical colleges.[15]

This initiative was followed by the Evangelical Youth Climate Initiative (EYCI), released in November 2006, which featured over 1,500 signatures by student leaders from across the United States. The EYCI was launched at a press conference and lobbying effort in Washington, D.C., which is how fellow Wheaton representative Jennifer Luedtke and I ended up dressed in uncomfortably formal suits, dashing toward the Capitol Building in the pouring rain. We had helped collect signatures for the EYCI from our classmates and had come as representatives to deliver them to our Illinois senators—Dick Durbin and Barack Obama. The guards at the security checkpoint chuckled sympathetically as we dripped through the metal detectors with blue ink running off our notes.

Once through, we made a beeline for the bathrooms and decimated their stock of recycled paper towels patting ourselves down (not my most earth-friendly moment of the day). Now damp instead of drenched, we met up with our peers from Trinity Christian College (Palos Heights, Illinois) and had a short but pleasant meeting with staffers for the senators. I don't know how much impact our visit had on them, especially since our senators were already advocating for strong environmental policies. Still, we hoped that being there helped remind our politicians that Christians care about creation and are actively paying attention to how the government treats the earth.

The EYCI eventually led to the Wheaton Summit on Creation Care, organized and hosted by a student team at Wheaton College in January 2007. The summit brought together peers from fifteen other campuses to meet with Sir John Houghton and to learn from one another and key senior leaders within the creation care movement (more on this in chapter ten).

This flurry of attention and activity did not go unnoticed. A Christian ethicist in Florida named Calvin Beisner quickly responded to the original ECI statement and rallied another group of leaders to release a counter-statement under the auspices of the Interfaith Stewardship Alliance. Their reactionary document, "A Call to Truth, Prudence, and Protection of the Poor: An Evangelical Response to Global Warming," did little to diminish the ECI's effectiveness, however, and represents a dwindling minority.[16] This changing tune among Christians was also picked up by prominent secular members of the scientific community, who began turning to the church for help. Desperate to save the planet, but not making enough progress on their own, they have started to view the church as a powerful new ally.

Their message is that, while we may not agree with each other on how the planet came to exist, we all agree that we need to take better care of it. Christians responded to their overtures, and leaders from the National Association of Evangelicals and the Center for Health and the Global Environment at Harvard Medical School organized meetings. Finally, early in 2007, representatives from the evangelical and scientific communities held a news conference in Washington, D.C., to release the "Urgent Call to Action" and announce a joint effort to protect the environment.[17] Reverend Ken Wilson, one of the signatories of this document and the senior pastor at the Ann Arbor Vineyard Church, teamed us with renowned ocean conservationist Carl Safina to further develop this collaborative effort into "The Friendship Project." The goal of The Friendship Project is "to foster relationship and dialogue between scientists and evangelicals who share a common concern for the environment."[18]

Then, in a move that surprised many, members of the sixteen-million-strong Southern Baptist Convention independently released their groundbreaking Southern Baptist Environment and Climate Initiative (SBECI) in March 2008.[19] Even though some key leaders' names do not yet appear on the document at the time of this writing, three former convention presidents along with the incumbent president are original signatories. Jonathan Merritt, a young seminarian and upcoming leader, spearheaded the SBECI itself, which represents a big step for a denomination that has typically been, by its own admission, slow on the uptake with creation care issues.

These various initiatives, from the Evangelical Declaration on the Care of Creation to the SBECI have a tangible prophetic sense to them; their leaders are going out on a limb to apply their positions of influence toward awakening the church at large on creation care issues.

They are not alone. Each of these initiatives have been built on the solid foundations established by grassroots movements over the years. They are but the latest of many promising signs that the church is recovering a more biblical and holistic mission as we face a warming planet.

Uplink: Vince Morris, Risk Manager, Wheaton College

One of the great puzzles of American evangelicalism is, Why aren't we at the forefront of creation care movements?

Our doctrines of creation, fall, redemption and sanctification are a snug, natural fit with love for and care of God's creation, and indeed the Bible tells us our first instructions from God were to care for his creation as his imagers on earth (see Gen 1:26; 2:15). Through Christ's redemptive work, our relationships can be healed with God, with humans—and with the rest of creation. Otherwise, what does that "all things" mean in Colossians 1:20? How can Romans 8:21 say creation "will be liberated"? Yet rarely do evangelicals deliberate proper stewardship (beyond financial) and how to practice it. When is the last time you heard a sermon on creation care?

A proper environmental stewardship does not abandon traditional evangelistic and social concerns, nor is it a prioritization of creatures over humans; rather, it recognizes that our neglect of this area of theology has had profound negative consequences, and it considers how best to join in this part of Christ's reconciliation.

With this need in mind, I became the first chairperson of Wheaton College's fledgling Environmental Stewardship Advisory Committee in 2005. Since then Wheaton has not quite yet become a beacon of stewardship, but there are serious and hopeful conversations—and actions—taking place at an institutional level that demonstrate what considered creation care can and should look like.

In the frigid January 2007, another sign of spring burst forth: the student-led Wheaton Summit on Creation Care described briefly by Ben in this chapter. I was privileged to observe some of evangelicalism's bright new lights begin to shine as intense, thoughtful and energized students from around the country discussed both theoretical and practical ways to turn the old evangelical battleship toward this new compass heading. Perhaps Wheaton College—and, as more and more signs indicate, the rest of evangelicalism—is beginning to take seriously our creation care mandate after all.

Since I spent a decade as a youth minister, a favorite quotation is from Dr. James Plueddemann, chairman of missions and evangelism at Trinity Evangelical Divinity School: "There is no greater joy in life than watching the maturing process of people you care about." This is true, whether those folks are enthusiastic students dreaming big at a summit or mature Christians encountering a whole new area of God's restoration work.

5

Spheres of Change
Where This Movement Is Germinating

If future generations are to remember us more with gratitude than sorrow, we must achieve more than just the miracles of technology. We must also leave them a glimpse of the world as it was created, not just as it looked when we got through with it.

Lyndon B. Johnson

Have you spent time in a greenhouse?

My parents both like gardening, so when spring finally reaches New England, they spend an inordinate amount of time wandering through nursery greenhouses to stock up for the season. It is hot, stuffy and steamy inside. But plants, especially young ones, grow much healthier and faster in this sheltered environment. Greenhouses stay nice and warm, and plants in them receive lots of light, water and all the right nutrients to help them grow strong and get a head start on the season. So farmers and nurseries often start their plants as seedlings in greenhouses and nurture them until they are strong enough to be transplanted out into the big growing fields—or sold to my parents.

The Analogy

We have metaphorical equivalents for nurturing and developing Christians—especially younger ones—so that we can live well in the "real world." Our communities are our greenhouses: churches, colleges and universities, seminaries and fellowship groups. These are the fertile soil where seeds of the creation care movement are planted. We come together in these venues, ready to grow and eager to learn how to make the world a better place. They are high-energy training grounds, filled with hope and charged by our idealism.

A lot of good conservation work can be modeled in such settings.

These communities vary widely in size, resembling anything from a large household to a small city. Either way, they all use resources and energy, and are prime models for testing and showcasing sustainability practices.

As creation care becomes a priority in our core communities, it quickly expands outward. Consider college campuses and church youth groups. Every year, accomplished graduates disperse all around the world—carrying a concern for creation care with them. As they head out, new recruits come in to replace them, and the cycle continues. Not only does this help spread the movement like wildfire, but it also helps sustain it by continually raising up fresh faces and culturally relevant perspectives.

Or take churches, for example. The fifty to five thousand of us in any given church on Sunday morning spend the rest of the week scattered all across society, where we can have great influence for good in our home, business, government office or corporation.

As greenhouses are key to a healthy harvest, campuses and churches are key to an effective movement.

The Experience

Three weeks, five states, twenty-one meetings—and a two-seater hybrid car to get us through it all. In October 2007, Matthew Sleeth and I hit the road for A Rocha on an educational tour that took us all over the Northeast. Wherever we stopped, we found warm hospitality, good food and encouraging signs that the movement to care for creation is healthy and growing on all fronts.

Churches. Sunday, September 30. I left my Chicago apartment at 4 a.m. and drove to Dayton, Ohio, to meet up with Matthew and his wife, Nancy. We met at Westminster Presbyterian Church, right in the heart of Dayton, where Matthew spoke to an overflowing adult Sunday school class. This event, hosted by the new Earth Stewardship Ministry Team, included volunteers within the congregation who had read Matthew's *Serve God, Save the Planet* and were brainstorming ways to green up their church.

Churches are particularly important in the movement, because this is where we regularly come together to study the Bible and learn what it means to live and grow in community. They consume a lot of resources, which makes them easy targets for conservation. Also, churches are usually planted in the same neighborhood for many years, where they can develop lasting relationships and initiate long-term projects to impact the local community.

Ideas for projects include developing the church grounds into a natural area that welcomes both the neighbors and native wildlife, participating in community supported agriculture or community gardens, training volunteer "green teams" to help lower-income residents retrofit their homes with energy-efficient appliances that will save money and pollution, organizing community-wide tree-planting celebrations every Earth Day, or just providing bike racks and lockers to encourage churchgoers to bike, blade or walk to church.

Many other churches are moving forward as Westminster Presbyterian is. Churchgoers usually come across an outside resource—often a book or article—and gain a vision for environmental stewardship. They then share this resource and vision with others in the congregation, including the pastoral staff.

This can lead to opportunities to engage more of the church through creation care Bible studies, Sunday school series and sermons. As interest and enthusiasm build, the next step is often to form creation care ministries or a task force like the one at Westminster. For some churches, this ministry may fit under a broader social concerns committee instead of standing alone. Either way, the purpose of this group is to help the church keep a focus on creation care concerns and make practical changes toward being better stewards of creation.

Another way churches can get involved is from the top—when the pastoral staff takes the initiative to make creation care a priority. This was more the case at Northland, A Church Distributed in Longwood, Florida. Its senior pastor, Joel Hunter, is a board member of the National Association of Evangelicals and was the face and voice in a television promotion for the Evangelical Climate Initiative. Because of his preaching and personal involvement in creation care efforts, members of the church came together to form a task force uniquely named Creation, I Care.[1]

Youth groups. We had to hit the road soon after the Sunday school meeting at Westminster Presbyterian. Matthew kissed his wife goodbye, and we took off in my car. Our next stop was a youth group talk at Grace United Methodist Church in Grove City, Pennsylvania.

We arrived at Grace just in time to join the youth group for dinner, followed by a game where two teams competed to build the best sailing ship out of recyclable materials. After a winner was declared and the ships were enthusiastically demolished, Matthew and I tag-teamed on an interactive talk that started with showing a short film and ended with a good chunk of time for questions and answers. Q&A can be a lot of fun in youth groups and often ends with random questions like "When the earth becomes too polluted to live on, which planet would you choose to move to and why?"

Youth groups are a key component to the movement because this is where discipleship starts for many of us. What we learn here helps lay our faith foundation and build a Christian framework for interpreting and changing the world around us.

They also often wield untapped potential for influencing church policy, priorities and practices through parents and the youths' own example. A youth group I was involved with once petitioned the church leaders to do away with disposable cups for refreshments after the service. This really caught the attention of the elder board.

Imagine the compelling message that gets across if the youth all pitch in to replace light bulbs in the sanctuary with compact fluorescent models, donate recycled paper for printing the Sunday bulletins or get their hands dirty by cleaning up the church grounds and starting a vegetable garden. Such sacrificial acts of service will be noticed and could inspire the whole church to embark on a journey toward good environmental stewardship.

Christian campuses. Over the next couple of days, Matthew and I stayed in the area for events at Grove City College, an academically rigorous liberal arts institution with a strong commitment to the evangelical faith.

Grove City College has a picturesque campus with impressive

architecture and meticulous landscaping. In the center is an open quad lined at one end by stately trees that slope down to Wolf Creek, where students and professors hold annual streambed cleanups and native plant restoration efforts. Other than this, however, the campus culture had traditionally been disengaged from environmental stewardship. That is, until about 2005, when a small group of students came together to form the Grove City Environmental Club, or Eclub for short. They found enthusiastic support from a few staff and faculty, including the chaplain, who agreed to hold chapel talks on creation care.

This is how Matthew and I came into the picture. Matthew addressed the whole student body during the main chapel service, and during an alternative chapel session in the evening I shared about how I came to care about environmental issues. We spent much of the in-between times hanging out with members of the Eclub and resident life staff.

The Eclub was a small group, but we were very impressed with their good cheer and strong commitment to cultivating a culture of environmental stewardship around them. Eclub volunteers were at first responsible for gathering most of the dorm recycling and trucking it to a local recycling center. Over time, the student-led recycling program took hold, and the amount of materials greatly increased. Their efforts really paid off in 2008 when the college agreed to take over responsibility for the program. Off campus, Eclub partners with nonprofit organizations like PA Cleanways and the Salvation Army to clear broken appliances, old tires and other trash from illegal dumping grounds around the community.

Christian schools like Grove City have a central role to play in mobilizing the church to care for creation, because these are often the trendsetters in the church. As we grapple with contemporary issues and moral problems like global warming, churches look to Christian colleges for wisdom and leadership. After all, this is where a great deal of the scholarship, research, writing and organizing happens. That is why it is highly significant that so many Christian college presidents have signed on to the Evangelical Climate Initiative.

Even so, many Christian campuses trail their secular counterparts in environmental stewardship. Fifty-seven out of the 105 member colleges of the Council of Christian Colleges and Universities (CCCU) are now affiliated with the Au Sable Institute of Environmental Studies, but just under half of the 105 CCCU member institutions' websites list either their own environmental studies majors or biology majors with an environmental track.[2] Only two campuses—Goshen College and Taylor University (both in Indiana)—offer graduate degrees in environmental fields.

It appears that a majority of Christian campuses also do not have active environmental clubs or established venues where students, staff and faculty can pursue creation care discussion and action. Among colleges that do have such venues, there's a lack of cross-campus communication and cooperation, and most student environmental groups still function as isolated and independent entities that are often marginalized and limited in their impact.

The good news is that a lot of this seems to be changing. For instance, in 2008 John Brown University (Arkansas) announced a new bachelor's degree in renewable energy, and Lipscomb University (Tennessee) launched their Institute for Sustainable Practice. Activism is also increasing in this next generation and, as I will continue to share, new initiatives are popping up on campuses all the time.

Here is some arithmetic: as of 2008, there are 105 member institutions of the CCCU and 77 nonmember affiliate schools in 24 countries. Therefore, it's probably safe to say that there are more than 400,000 students enrolled at CCCU member and affiliate institutions every year. (This is surely the case if we include enrollment at denominational schools that have not affiliated with the CCCU.) Using back-of-the-napkin calculations, this means about 100,000 young Christians are commissioned every year from these schools and another 100,000 new students enroll.

If we reach every person on these campuses with the creation care message before they graduate, imagine the huge impact this will have on the church and the world. This does not even take into account the impact students can already have while still in college or the long-term influence the faculty and staff of these institutions have within Christian culture and their own communities.

Other campuses. There is also a lot of potential for change on secular campuses, though there has so far been even less environmental engagement by Christians within these contexts. According to the U.S. Department of Higher Education, there are more than four thousand degree-granting institutions of higher education in the United States. Many of these schools are showing tremendous leadership in pursuing sustainability.

The Association for the Advancement of Sustainability in Higher Education is a nonprofit umbrella organization that serves as a huge resource and information clearinghouse for campus sustainability efforts across the United States.[3] It also partners with the Sustainable Endowments Institute to produce the College Sustainability Report Card, an independent evaluation of the top two hundred campuses in terms of endowment size.

The Sustainable Endowments Institute reports that there is a wave of institutional support building to address the sustainability challenge:

> The results [of the 2008 Report Card] clearly show a "green groundswell" on campuses, with nearly 45 percent of colleges committing to fight climate change through cutting carbon emissions. High-performance green building standards guide new construction at 59 percent of schools, while 42 percent are using hybrid or electric vehicles in transportation fleets. Notably, 37 percent of schools purchase renewable energy and 30 percent produce their own wind or solar energy. A substantial 70 percent buy food from local farms and 64 percent serve fair trade coffee.[4]

The report card gave 25 of these 200 schools the highest overall grade of A-, including Harvard (Massachusetts), Dartmouth (New Hampshire), University of Washington, Middlebury (Vermont), Carleton (Minnesota) and University of Vermont. Wheaton College, the only CCCU member that qualified for the survey, received a C-, while the Baptist-affiliated Samford University (Alabama) scored an F. Secular institutions that are regularly cited by other rankings as leaders in sustainability efforts include College of the Atlantic (Maine), University of Maryland, Yale University (Connecticut), Oberlin College (Ohio), University of Washington and Berea College (Kentucky), to name a few.[5]

A lot of this aptly termed "green groundswell" comes from the students themselves. Penn State students successfully campaigned for their university to implement a comprehensive climate policy that includes ten million dollars of efficiency improvements every year, a minimum 20-percent wind energy purchase and LEED (Leadership in Energy and Environmental Design) certification for all new construction. Student groups on other campuses have implemented popular bike-sharing programs, raised money to purchase solar panels or wind energy and encouraged their presidents to sign the American College and University Presidents Climate Commitment.

The above achievements have mostly come from environmental groups such as the Sierra Student Coalition and the National Wildlife Federation's Campus Ecology Program. But many of these campuses also have active parachurch ministries like InterVarsity Christian Fellowship (IVCF) or Campus Crusade for Christ. This opens up three distinct but not mutually exclusive avenues for engagement by Christians.

The first is to work within existing ministries like IVCF to develop a culture of creation care that will influence how the group operates and reaches out to the wider campus community. However, while it may be manageable to plan a large-group talk on creation care—as many IVCF chapters are doing—most staff and student leaders are too stretched with existing ministry obligations to create a longer-term focus on specific issues like creation care.

The second option is to start a distinctly Christian environmental initiative or group. This will likely be hard on most secular campuses, where it can be challenging to find a sizable group of Christians who are also passionately focused on creation care. Under the right conditions, however, it can happen. Ohio State University is the largest university in the United States, with more than sixty thousand students enrolled in 2008. In recent years, involvement in their campus environmental club has skyrocketed, and Christian participants started discussing the possibility of planting a partner group that will continue to promote sustainability on campus but from a distinctly Christian perspective. Their hopes are slowly starting to take form, thanks to enthusiastic responses from the existing environmental club's leadership, along with the strong support of Greg Hitzhusen, a Christian professor who specializes in ecotheology.

The third avenue for engagement is simply to get involved in existing environmental initiatives. This is what Jonathan Bosma ended up doing at Michigan Tech University. Jon was a forestry major who tried repeatedly to start a Christian environmental group on campus. He had trouble finding a professor who was able to serve as an adviser, however, and many of the Christian peers he knew were already heavily committed to other ministries. So, in the end, he chose to get involved with the mainstream environmental efforts already active on his campus—and ended up making lasting friendships along the way.

Communities. By this point on our educational tour, Matthew and I had already been in Grove City for a few busy but very rewarding days. The last event in the area was a community gathering hosted by JusticeWorks Ministries, an ecumenical group of Christians from Grove City area churches.

This thoughtfully planned event included delicious home-baked desserts; fair-trade, shade-grown coffee; and a resource table with ways to practice creation care and information on various local environmental initiatives. Another table offered cloth shopping bags and relevant books for sale at discounted rates for those who wanted to learn more after we finished speaking. Attendance that evening was good, with a diverse crowd from multiple churches and generations coming to fellowship and learn together.

Christian groups that address environmental issues within churches and campuses are more common than those that work in local residential communities, such as JusticeWorks Ministries. Again, however, this is changing. Entrepreneurial community groups are springing up literally all across the United States. As I write, A Rocha USA has new community groups in Seattle, Washington; Santa Barbara, California; Lynden,

Dispatch: A Rocha Santa Barbara

Our green neighborhood community group is up and running! Six of us from Santa Barbara Community Church have met regularly and dreamed together about what it would look like to do community-based outreach that would encourage people to work together, look at their lifestyles and change their energy consumption habits. We are working in Santa Barbara's Westside, where we all live.

Our first neighborhood event was a barbeque drop-in party. We were happy to meet neighbors we'd never known before and reconnect with others. Thirty adults stopped by for good food and conversation. We asked every person to fill out a survey asking if they would be interested in learning more about energy-efficient lighting, composting, gardening and recycling. Using the data we collected, we will plan informational seminars. We also hope to meet again for hikes and local creek cleanup days, or just to fellowship with others who care about creation. We are most excited about loving our neighbors—helping create community and a sense of responsibility right here in our neighborhood.

We also were able to host a table at the Santa Barbara Surfrider Foundation's annual Paddle Out, a show of solidarity among the surfing community for improved water quality along our coast. With around two hundred people participating, we had some good conversations with fellow Santa Barbarans who care about protecting our waters.

Finally, we are excited to be working alongside our neighborhood elementary school and a nearby church to help establish organic gardens that will provide produce for school lunches and lower-income families in our area. We can't wait to see where things will go from here.

Washington; Fredericksburg, Texas; Wilmore, Kentucky; and Boise, Idaho. There are also preexisting or newly developing community initiatives in other states that AR is considering partnerships with.

Many of these are volunteer groups with a dual mission to mobilize local churches and to serve the broader community. Wilmore Creation Care in Kentucky has started community garden plots at a local church and helps to coordinate ongoing recycling efforts at Ichthus, the Christian music festival in Wilmore every summer.

Others, like AR Santa Barbara, started with volunteers but has a long-term vision to hire staff and set up a field center.

In addition to these practical projects, community groups like AR Santa Barbara and Wilmore Creation Care are valuable because they help strengthen communities by sharing fun and fellowship through potlucks, prayer meetings, hymn singing and field trips to local natural areas. Potential remains for the formation of synergistic relationships with nearby campuses or mainstream environmental groups like local Sierra Club chapters. Both AR Santa Barbara and Wilmore Creation Care often collaborate on organic gardening projects with the A Rocha student chapters at Westmont College and Asbury College, respectively.

Seminaries. After a few memorable days in Grove City, it was time for Matthew and me to hit the road again. Energized by our meaningful visit and supplied with generous care packages from our hosts, we drove east to Drew University (Madison, New Jersey), where Matthew gave another chapel talk.

Our host was Laurel Kearns, a professor of environmental studies at Drew Theological School. Laurel is also on the steering committee for the Green Seminary Initiative, an effort to encourage environmental stewardship at seminaries and promote what campuses are doing through a central clearinghouse website.[6]

I was surprised to find a professor of environmental studies in a theological school. Most evangelical seminaries do not even have classes on creation care theology, let alone programs or positions in this specific field. Garrett-Evangelical Theological Seminary in Chicago runs a Theology of Creation course, while others, such as Eastern Mennonite

Seminary (Harrisonburg, Virginia) and Fuller Seminary (Pasadena, California) offer Christian ethics and systematic theology courses with creation care modules integrated into the curriculum.

Richard Mouw, the president of Fuller Seminary, also signed on to the Evangelical Climate Initiative and is an outspoken advocate of action to address climate change. In 2006, the campus newsletter dedicated one of its weekly editions to creation care and featured interviews with Jim Ball of the Evangelical Environmental Network and alumnus Rob Bell from Mars Hill Bible Church in Michigan.

Still, there is a lot of room for growth here.

I have been going to church all my life, but it was not until my freshman year in college that I finally heard a sermon about caring for creation. This is certainly not unusual; most pastors have not received any training in this area. Given how important creation care is in Christian discipleship, wouldn't it be good for all seminary graduates to have a foundation in creation care theology that is at least strong enough for them to preach a sermon from?

It will take creativity to make this work within already packed core requirements, but options include integrating special seminars, new classes or even just readings in creation care throughout the relevant parts of the curriculum.

In his book *Our Father's World,* Ed Brown makes a good point about the critical role seminaries play in the environmental crisis:

> Few people will exert more influence for good or for ill than the leaders of tomorrow's congregations. And we know exactly where these future leaders are: They are in class right now, in Bible college and seminary. They are studying Greek and Hebrew and homiletics and systematic theology and counseling and youth ministry and . . . almost everything but environmental theology or creation care.[7]

The Journey Continues

After Drew Theological School, Matthew and I parted ways for a week. He drove down to Washington, D.C., to join other evangelical leaders in lobbying Congress on climate action. I hopped a train up to Boston to spend time with family and catch up on backlogged e-mails.

We were only a third of the way into the tour so far. Before it was over we would make stops in Massachusetts at Gordon College, Andover Newton Theological Seminary, the Chinese Bible Church of Greater Boston and the L'Abri community in Southborough, and in New York at Houghton College—all of which are taking important steps forward in caring for creation. At the end, we would return to our homes exhausted but greatly encouraged with how God is working through a creation care movement that is organically sprouting up and bearing fruit at every turn.

Uplink: Paul Corts, President, Council for Christian Colleges and Universities

The Role of Christian Higher Education in Creation Care

Ben Lowe's analogy that Christian colleges are the "greenhouses" of the church is (pardon the pun) truly fertile. A central mission of Christian higher education is to cultivate a Christian view of all things—as Paul succinctly states, to "take captive every thought" to Christ (2 Cor 10:5). Christian institutions of higher education are "thought centers" for Christianity. They are responsible both to pass down (to tend and nurture, following Lowe's analogy) the great inheritance of our faith and to think anew (to germinate and grow) what that faith means to every aspect of life, including our natural lives as organisms in a complex, global ecosystem.

Yet, as Lowe points out, Christian colleges have been late to "plow the fields" of creation care. While such thought centers have for many decades rightly called Christians to address human-to-human injustices like racism and violence, Christian colleges have only more recently become active with developing care of the creation (human-to-environment concerns) as a central mandate of our faith.

That does not mean, in my view at least, that Christian higher education had no regard for the care of creation. Rather central to its mission of taking all things captive in Christ is the notion that we are called to be "stewards" of creation—literally, one who manages another's property, a "ward" or keeper of something that one does not own oneself but is entrusted to preserve and grow. As stewards, we are responsible to lead by example, to model stewarding behavior for the college-age cohort but also for the broader Christian church and wider culture.

So while Christian higher education over the past century didn't disregard creation care, it also seems fair to claim that, as Lowe argues, it didn't emphasize it either. But Christian higher education over the past decade is developing our *implicit* notions of creation stewardship into more *explicit* directives of creation care. Christian colleges are increasingly becoming aware of their responsibilities as energy consumers, as moral educators of future leaders and as microcosms of environmental sustainability. Our implicit notion of creation stewardship can no longer remain implicit, assumed or hidden, but now must become our explicit work, demonstrating our care for the earth that God has given us but that we do not own.

What unique contribution then can Christian higher education make to this emerging, explicit work of creation care? As thought centers for Christianity, Christian colleges can provide a clear and forceful vision of why care of creation is central to participating in God's work in the world. Christian colleges can also give courage to the creation care movement, to embolden the future generations of the church to work for a sustainable future. Christian higher education can imaginatively shape the discussion of this important topic so that subsequent generations will know that we were faithful stewards of God's gifts to us—intellectual, spiritual and, yes, the very gift of creation itself. And we can work to develop sustainable practices for our campuses that will be a testimony to our commitment. May those of us who work in the greenhouse of Christian higher education have the moral vision, courage and imagination to do nothing less and yet much more.

6

Transformation
A Movement of Change

What good is it, my brothers, if a man claims to have faith but has no deeds? Can such faith save him? . . . I will show you my faith by what I do.

James 2:14, 18

The 2,500-member Vineyard Boise is an evangelical church that has made a big difference in its community when it comes to creation care. It has been featured in numerous articles and films, including the 2006 "Is God Green?" PBS special with Bill Moyers.[1] Senior Pastor Tri Robinson has published two creation care books and is a sought-after speaker on the topic.[2]

But it has not always been this way.

Authentic Change

As recently as 2005, no one had any reason to hear of Vineyard Boise in association with the environment. Being a conservative congregation in ranch country, they expressed few fuzzy feelings toward what was perceived as liberal environmentalism. All this changed when Tri had a personal reawakening to the biblical mandate of creation care. He wrestled with this issue in the Bible for six months before finally getting up to preach a sermon about it.

Tri was worried how his congregation would react to his sermon; he received a standing ovation in all three services. Since then, the church has put its faith into action by applying this recovered vision for creation care throughout its community. It created a ministry called Let's Tend the Garden to help coordinate new programs like Tithe Your Trash, a campaign where people brought their recyclables to church where they had sorting bins. They even raised about ten thousand dollars from old cell phones donated for recycling.

Over time, the church switched to using recycled paper and biodegradable coffee cups. Members regularly partner with the Forest Service to plant trees, clear trails and remove invasive species from nearby protected areas. Let's Tend the Garden has organized an annual conference focusing on creation care since 2006, and maintains a website that provides helpful information on their activities.[3] They also tend a garden on the church grounds that annually produces 13,000 pounds of fresh produce for lower-income families in the surrounding community.

Vineyard Boise has taken bold beginning steps toward changing the way they live as individuals and as a church. When I asked Tri about the inspiring transformation they are undergoing, he replied,

> We believe Christians should be the most concerned about the preservation of the environment because God's people were the first to be commissioned to care for his creation. We refer to this as the "covenant of the rainbow." In Genesis 9 God said, "When I see the rainbow in the clouds, I will remember the eternal covenant between God and every living creature on earth." We do this not because of Mother Earth but because it belongs to Father God.[4]

He makes a good point. Everything we do—and often what we do not do—sends a message about who we are and what we care about. How we live betrays what we truly value and what we really believe.

The purpose of movements like Vineyard Boise and numerous others is to renew our hearts and minds, and transform every aspect of how we live together on this earth to more authentically reflect our belief in a God who created the world, loves it and calls us to do the same: "Do not conform any longer to the pattern of this world, but be transformed by the renewing of your mind. Then you will be able to test and approve what God's will is—his good, pleasing and perfect will" (Rom 12:2).

Levels of Change

What can this look like? There are two basic levels of transformation: people can be changed and structures can be changed.

Individual or personal change is very important. Tri was changed through studying what the Bible said about tending the garden, just as hearing him preach about it changed his congregation. This led them to take practical steps, such as bringing recyclables to church and volunteering with the Forest Service.

There is also great power in systemic change, such as when Vineyard Boise switched to using recycled paper and biodegradable coffee cups. The way our social structures are set up has a large influence on our behavior and can even override sincerely held beliefs.

InterVarsity Press editor Al Hsu was reminded of this while attending a conference that did not have recycling bins. He said, "Even though most of us were committed recyclers, it was all too easy to toss stuff when there weren't recycling bins around. One of my colleagues actually took all of her empty plastic water bottles back home in her luggage rather than throw them away in the regular trash, which would have been much easier."[5]

As Al said, people did care about their impact on the earth, but the structures around them made it inconvenient to live out their commitments. A systemic change—making recycling bins available throughout the conference center—would have resulted in many of the attendees recycling.

Similarly, while many people are happy to save paper, they usually don't make the effort to program their copiers or printers to print on both sides of a sheet. An effective systemic change here would be for offices and libraries to set the default setting on their machines to double-sided.

Eastern Mennonite University (EMU) has been working hard to implement systemic change on campus for many years. They have been pioneers in constructing energy-efficient buildings and installing innovative heating and cooling systems since the 1980s. In 2007, they were ranked third out of ninety colleges and universities surveyed for efficient energy use by the Association of Higher Education Facilities Officers. Thanks to their efficient systems, EMU currently spends only 469 dollars per student per year in energy bills, which is less than half of what most colleges their size spend. EMU also composts food waste in a partnership between the Earthkeepers student group and the food service provider. Earthkeepers even raised a few pigs off some of the scraps (the pigs were named Sallie Mae, Pork Chop and Tenderloin).[6]

Another compelling example of structural change comes from Abilene Christian University (Texas). They save more than 85 million gallons of water every year by recycling effluent water to irrigate the more than two thousand native trees they have planted to beautify their campus.[7] They also installed low-flow showerheads and toilets to further conserve water use in the dry climate.

Levers of Change

How does change like what's described above happen? How can we motivate people beyond concern and on to action? How can we encourage actual transformation?

Consider the following five distinct "levers" when looking to effect meaningful change.[8] This list is not exhaustive, and each of these levers has its own strengths and weaknesses. Holistic approaches to transformation often involve a combination of most, if not all, of them.

Education. We learn new information that helps us reevaluate a situation, resulting in a new outcome or decision. For example, many college food services now consider sustainable fisheries in their seafood choices. Some check the Monterey Bay Aquarium Seafood Watch and will not serve fish that come from the "avoid" list.[9] One year they may serve farmed Atlantic salmon but the next year they might replace it with farmed tilapia because the former was higher on the watch list. Education is an important lever, but it alone usually does not motivate change.

Mandates. We are required to change by a higher authority; there are often penalties for not complying. For instance, some grocery stores do not give out free plastic or paper bags anymore. Either customers bring their own bags from home or they have to transfer loose groceries from the cart into their car. Mandates can be useful, but do not reflect a true change of heart—at least in the beginning—and sometimes require costly enforcement in order to be effective.

Peer pressure. We often do things to be affirmed by others or because everyone else is doing it and we want to fit in. For instance, a few families at church start taking their kids camping together, and soon other families feel compelled to go camping as well. Peer pressure can be an especially effective lever within communities and can provide normative expectations that encourage us to do good and avoid taking shortcuts.

Economics. We choose the option that carries the highest cost-benefit ratio in our favor. Trucks and SUVs used to be all the rage, but when gas prices skyrocketed to above four dollars per gallon, more people switched to smaller cars and hybrid models. Economics has been the key for making progress in the environmental movement so far. While this is an important lever, it is not enough on its own and leaves little room for making meaningful financial sacrifices.

Morality. We do something because it is right. The physical plant at Palm Beach Atlantic University (Florida) now uses only eco-friendly cleaning chemicals and methods and has implemented an award-winning recycling program for paper, cardboard, plastic, metals, batteries, and fluorescent lamps and ballasts. Their staff decided that good environmental stewardship is a priority and well worth the hassle of implementing these changes.

There are many ways that these five levers work well together, and it is valuable to consider which would be most relevant within each specific context.

In 2003, Eastern University (Pennsylvania) became the first CCCU school to switch over to 100-percent wind energy on a main campus. This achievement was made possible only because of a creative grassroots campaign that pulled three out of the five levers—and then a fourth one later. Investing in this much wind energy would cost students an optional, additional fee of twenty-two dollars. Signing students up for optional fees like this can be a hard sell, even if it's only twenty-two dollars a semester. But Eastern is well known for its holistic view of the gospel, which emphasizes social justice issues like creation care.

Advocates for the wind-energy project tapped into this institutional identity by drawing the connections between wind energy, less pollution and a healthier planet—the education and moral levers. They also gathered signatures for petitions in person, adding an element of peer pressure to the campaign. Since then, support for the program has grown on campus while the wind-energy market has become more established and financially competitive—the economic lever.

At the same time, though, true transformation does not come from coercion, guilt trips, greed or self-righteousness, but from hearts and minds that are being sanctified by the Holy Spirit. The Spirit is the ultimate agent of change. Unlike the above, however, the Holy Spirit is not a lever that we pull, but a powerful movement from God that we can be open to and earnestly pray for.

This is not to suggest that the other levers do not play an important and legitimate role in encouraging meaningful progress. They do. But there is something far greater and more mysterious going on behind the scenes. Even as we intentionally strategize our approach to bringing about change, the priority must always be to make room for the Spirit to continually orient us toward God and his good desires. The rest follows.

Living Our Change

Tolstoy famously declared, "Everybody wants to change the world, but no one thinks of changing himself." Any call to transformation must first begin with ourselves. Integrity is scarce. We see this clearly in politics and, sadly, in the church as well. Far too many people have taken a strong public position on an issue, only to be found living in contradiction to their words. The logic flows that if their message is too weak to change their lives, how can it change ours? Jesus asks—and answers—this same question:

> Why do you look at the speck of sawdust in your brother's eye and pay no attention to the plank in your own eye? How can you say to your brother, "Let me take the speck out of your eye," when all the time there is a plank in your own eye? You hypocrite, first take the plank out of your own eye, and then you will see clearly to remove the speck from your brother's eye. (Mt 7:3-5; see also Lk 6:41-42)

Integrity counts. If we want to be listened to, we first need to practice what we preach; if we advocate taking care of the environment, we had better make sure our lives match up.

It was with this conviction in mind that my three roommates and I moved into our Chicago apartment together (as mentioned in chapter three). We were intentional about exploring ways to live simply and sustainably within our group, and here are some of the changes we made:

Power. We replaced all the old incandescent light bulbs with energy-efficient compact fluorescent bulbs (soft white) and made it a habit to turn off lights and unplug appliances (such as the microwave) when not in use. We do not own a TV, and we dry our laundry on an old-school clothesline instead of the dryer. As a result, we only use about one hundred to two hundred killowatt hours of electricity each month.

Water. We save water in many ways, including using a low-flow showerhead and showering together. Just kidding! While we are big on building community, we still take private showers. That said, I love long, hot showers but have now cut my shower time from around fifteen

Hanging clothes to dry in our Chicago apartment. Photo by Devin Ryan.

minutes to less than five. You can get cheap shower timers that stick to the walls to help keep track. I went another route. One of my favorite oldies songs is "Piano Man" by Billy Joel, which has a run time of about five and a half minutes. Perfect. I pushed play before getting in, and I make sure I am out of the shower by the time it ends.

Food. We try to eat lower on the food chain. This means more staples and produce and less meat. This has led us to set aside at least one day every week as a "meat fast." Sometimes we manage to snag some organic fruits and vegetables at reasonable prices, along with free-range eggs and fair-trade, shade-grown coffee. Besides being better for the planet, these dietary changes are also better for our health. Of course, any health benefits are easily offset when we get too busy or lazy to cook and end up eating instant noodles (which happens a lot).

Recycling. We have set up a "recycling center" in a corner of our kitchen for all our paper, plastic, glass and metal, which we take to a nearby recycling center. We also use recycled products—such as recycled toilet paper—when possible.

Other waste. We minimize paper usage, try to use recycled products and take our own cloth bags to the grocery store to cut down on plastic waste. We have not found a good way to compost in our city apartment yet (without using worms), but my family now composts at home, and it cuts down on a lot of trash. At first, I thought composting was complicated—and it can be if you want to get technical—but what works best for us is simply to box out a small area of the yard (a wood crate or a plastic tub with the bottom cut out works fine), dump the food scraps in, and throw some leaves or grass clippings over it all. If convenient, it helps to mix it up once in a while. The end. Before you know it, out comes great garden soil.

Cleaning products. Our laundry, dishwashing, bathroom and household cleaning soaps are all-natural and biodegradable—obtained on sale from our local supermarket.

Stuff. We rarely go shopping unless it is for groceries. All our furniture and most of our clothes are either hand-me-downs or come from thrift stores and yard sales—great reused stuff at really cheap prices. We also share many belongings with each other like a family would, which cuts down on how much we each need to own.

Hospitality. We try to emphasize hospitality by inviting friends and neighborhood folks over to share meals and fellowship. Besides building community, having friends over allows us to share the creation care message while modeling light living.

Travel. We all love to travel, and flying is my favorite way to get around, but it is also the worst for the planet. I drive a hybrid car provided by my work now, and I try to fly as little as possible. Hybrids are still expensive, but many other small cars get good mileage and cost a lot less. As a group, our household plans car trips to consolidate our grocery shopping and other errands. A further benefit to living in the city is that we can usually get around just by walking, biking or using public transportation.

Awareness. We watch for environmental issues in the news and share what we are learning with each other. And we're always experimenting with different ways of living "greener" lives.

Two Traps

We can fall into two traps when we pursue change, whether it's in ourselves or in the community around us. The first is that the changes we make can give us only the appearance of being environmentally sensible, while little below the surface is truly improved. In enviro-speak, this is called "greenwashing," and it can be either intentional or unintentional.[10]

For instance, we separate out the recyclables from our regular trash in public, but cut corners and dump both out together in private. Or we buy a fuel-efficient car but then end up driving it a lot more on unnecessary trips that were short enough to walk. In both scenarios, we are not as truly green as we think we are or give the appearance of being.

We must be alert to avoid greenwashing. We might make a change to help us look or feel good, instead of doing it because it really makes a difference. This can happen when we are not honest with those around us. Jesus railed at a group of religious leaders (the Pharisees) for trying to appear holy while living in sin:

> Woe to you, teachers of the law and Pharisees, you hypocrites! You are like whitewashed tombs, which look beautiful on the outside but on the inside are full of dead men's bones and everything unclean. In the same way, on the outside you appear to people as righteous but on the inside you are full of hypocrisy and wickedness. (Mt 23:27-28)

The second trap is legalism. This is something else the Pharisees struggled with. They were so busy keeping their rules that they lost track of the bigger picture; they emphasized the letter of the law so much that they did not grasp its meaning. As a result, they became self-righteous and prideful, judging and condemning others for not being as holy as themselves.

There are two aspects of this legalism. The first is that we end up obsessing about details and making them count far more than they really should. I often make this mistake. Once I got very involved in a discussion with some friends over whether it was more energy-efficient to boil water for tea in a hotpot or in a microwave—not a big deal compared to the cross-country roundtrip to Florida we were also planning. Many things we do in life affect the planet, but some have a far heavier impact than others. We should not get so distracted focusing on the little details that we miss the really big problems.

The second aspect of legalism is that it builds a superiority complex. In Luke 18, Jesus tells the parable of the Pharisee and the tax collector "to some who were confident of their own righteousness and looked down on everybody else" (v. 9). Retold in our context, the story might go something like this:

> Two men go to church one Sunday: an environmentalist and a business student. The environmentalist boldly stands up in public and thanks God that he is such a good person because of all he does to warn people about the environmental crisis: "I'm totally on top of this. I learn all about the damage going on in the planet. I fly

all over to see these places and buy lots of carbon credits to offset my travel. I am way ahead of the curve compared to everyone else!" In the corner, the business student bows his head and silently confesses, "I don't know very much about this environmental stuff yet, but I imagine my lifestyle is not sustainable at all. I wish I could afford a hybrid car or solar panels, and live close enough to bike to work, but I can't. I feel so trapped. I want to be a better steward of the earth—please help me."

Jesus concluded this parable—his original version—with a lesson that must have scandalized his audience: "I tell you that this man [the business student], rather than the other [the environmentalist], went home justified before God. For everyone who exalts himself will be humbled, and he who humbles himself will be exalted" (v. 14).

Legalism is a danger for all of us. We can get so caught up in the details of green living that we forget what really matters and begin to do things out of pride instead of love.

Learning to live well and sustainably on the earth is a lifelong process. I have found that being young is an advantage here, because I own relatively few material possessions and don't have a family yet. This is an easier time to be intentional about lifestyle choices and to start good habits that grow stronger through time.

In the end, though, we are all on this journey toward good stewardship together, even if we are at different stages or facing diverse circumstances along the way. The point here is not to compare or to compete with each other, but to keep moving in the right direction.

Along the way, other people will take notice and be inspired to join us on this journey. We are in a unique position to witness through the way we live. In a world inundated with many competing claims, actions speak louder than words, and transformed lives authenticate our message.

As Gandhi said, "You must be the change you want to see in the world."

Uplink: Bettie Ann Brigham, Vice President for Student Development, Eastern University

Justice begins with the recognition of the necessity of sharing.
Elias Canetti, Nobel Prize for Literature in 1981

Words for a World of Want
As a primary focus in the education of students, Eastern University has been concerned since its founding in 1925 with what happens in the world, to the earth and to all its people. Meanwhile, many seemingly similar institutions have spent decades of time and energy on such subjects as the acceptable length of their students' hair in the sixties and seventies, the number of earrings students were permitted to have in the eighties and nineties, and the timeless Christian conversational classic: "Should Christian students dance?"—a controversy that has been going strong, seemingly since the Beginning of Christian College Time. Eastern University has been different. It has stayed true to its simple but deeply profound mission of taking seriously what Jesus said. The clear challenge to the Eastern University community and to Christians everywhere is to, as President David Black says, "Read the red stuff," and thus use Jesus' actions, reactions and words as *the* ultimate model for interaction with other people, be they next door or across the oceans.

The university's motto "The Whole Gospel for the Whole World" has certainly been a challenging one, leading to long and involved discussions, exegesis, prayer, thought, more exegesis and more prayer whenever the community is faced with a tough decision that other Christian organizations might easily and offhandedly dismiss or avoid altogether. Long before it became an acronym on a wristband, "What would Jesus do?" has been and will continue to be the question asked daily at Eastern University. Asking the hard questions relative to how we should be in the world as Christians has resulted in answers and sometimes more questions and greater challenges to the Eastern University community. These challenges have spawned such dynamic people as Tony Campolo, Shane Claiborne, Bryan Stevenson, Jonathan Wilson-Hartgrove and many others less known but no less dedicated to the well-being of the earth and all inhabitants of it.

A few of the many, many actions that have been taken at Eastern University over the years in answer to this question involve investment portfolio examination and divestment; implementation of educational programs in cities and across the world to encourage and increase educational access; inviting the members of Soulforce Equality Ride to come and visit us, even before they officially announced the first "ride";

exclusive use of fair-trade coffee; implementation of easy-access programs for working adults; the use of wind energy for all electric power and so on.

Caring for others as Jesus did means caring for their health, their food sources, their well-being, their families and their communities, as well as their souls. Food for the soul can't be digested when the stomach is eating itself. Attention to the degradation of the environment that causes wild and unpredictable weather patterns now—and undeniably worsening and eventually more devastating impacts on global wellness later—is a natural focus for those who ask, "What would Jesus do?" The energy question came up early at Eastern and resulted in a conviction that we must act.

In 2003 Eastern students asked the question regarding the impending environmental crisis and decided that Jesus would certainly purchase wind energy. Why? It is clean, it is quiet, and its construction creates jobs for unskilled people. It does not emit toxins or chemical fumes, nor does it use dangerous chemicals. It does not have a half-life that needs to degrade for 24,360 years in order to stop killing people or stop dangerously modifying the DNA of living things. It does not require destruction of the environment, and it is from a resource that can never be used up as long as there is something called "weather" on

planet Earth. Wind is everywhere, so all people can have access to this energy source if they are given the tools. Probably the best part is that currently no one is fighting over wind; it can be neither fully owned nor controlled by powerful countries to exploit less powerful ones. Try as you might, you can't hold wind in your hands, yet you can harness its wondrous power to produce light and heat, two items essential for human civilization as we know it today.

And let's face it, most of the 6,774,501,940 people [11] who are living on planet Earth as I write this at 6:38 p.m. EST on January 2, 2008, are not going back to catching or harvesting their own food and living off the land.

In 2003 the work at Eastern began with a 25-percent commitment toward a five-year goal for the main campus at Eastern University to be 100-percent wind-energy sourced for all electric energy use. In the fall of 2006, more than a year early, the goal was accomplished.

The motto "The Whole Gospel for the Whole World" is an ambitious calling. The university's triad pillars—faith, reason and justice—add to the challenge of the call. Through prayer, discussion, exegesis, talk, thought, more prayer and earnest contemplation of Jesus' example for us, Eastern University will meet new challenges and find answers to the new questions to come. Will you join us?

7

Mustard Seed Organizing
How This Movement Grows

The kingdom of heaven is like a mustard seed, which a man took and planted in his field. Though it is the smallest of all your seeds, yet when it grows, it is the largest of garden plants and becomes a tree, so that the birds of the air come and perch in its branches.

Jesus (Mt 13:31-32)

In mid-summer 2006, author and environmental activist Bill McKibben had the idea to march fifty miles, from his home in Vermont to the state capitol, Burlington, in protest of Washington's inaction on climate change. A month later, after last-minute grassroots organizing, Bill and one thousand additional marchers walked through the streets of Burlington and rallied on the steps of the federal building.

Apparently, one thousand concerned citizens marching for five days in a line along Route 7 attracts a good bit of attention. Present to meet them at the rally were all the major state candidates for federal office that year. The marchers called on the candidates to take serious action on global warming by signing legislation proposed earlier in the summer by retiring U.S. Senator Jim Jeffords from Vermont.

And there, in front of press cameras, each of the candidates came up one by one and signed the bill—a compelling testimony to the power of mustard seed organizing. Bill McKibben reflects on what happened that day:

> What stood out was how easy it was to get agreement from even those candidates who had never made the issue a priority. It reminded me of a political truth that's easy to forget: you don't need everyone. You don't even need 51 percent. . . . 5 percent of the population is plenty to roll politicians as long as that 5 percent is committed, as long as that 5 percent is willing to get up and walk.[1]

Our efforts may start small and seem insignificant, but like the mustard seed, they can grow over time to have far-reaching impacts.

This is how creation care movements are developing today. They mostly start small and unglamorously with one person in a church, a couple of families in a neighborhood or a team of four on a campus of four thousand. But nothing is too small for God to accomplish his mighty purposes through. We read in the Bible that he used a small shepherd boy named David to defeat the mighty warrior Goliath and that Jesus used a mere five small loaves and two fish that one boy offered to feed five thousand hungry people, and they still had leftovers.

Why does he work this way? The apostle Paul gives one reason: "But God chose the foolish things of the world to shame the wise; God chose the weak things of the world to shame the strong. He chose the lowly things of this world and the despised things—and the things that are not—to nullify the things that are, so that no one may boast before him" (1 Cor 1:27-29).

God is not looking for greatness from us; he already has that covered himself. He has made it clear that what he wants is love and faithfulness. It is not that "big" is somehow "bad." Big is often good, but it is not the point here. We aren't expected to single-handedly stop global warming or save the Amazon rainforest tomorrow, but we all have to do our part. The point is being faithful to act with great love in *everything* God calls us to, even if it seems insignificant . . . like a mustard seed.

The rest of this chapter includes specific ideas from movements of Christians that are acting faithfully to protect creation in small ways, organizing and developing strategies that help them grow and impact their communities for good.

Mobilize. Every movement has to start somewhere, and the first step is to bring a core group of people together who are eager to explore what it means—and what it will take—to be better stewards of creation, both in their own lives and at the broader community level. This can be the beginning of a church small group or campus club.

When starting a grassroots group like this, there are two main logistical questions to work through: what kind of structural support would be helpful, and is there value here in affiliating with a larger organization?

First, organizational structure can seem like a bother, but it is a very necessary thing. For instance, hashing out a mission statement and goals helps the whole group articulate what it is about and what it is trying to do; putting together simple by-laws makes it clear to everyone how the group will work. On college campuses, it is invaluable to look for a good faculty or staff adviser as well. Advisers help student groups by sharing wisdom and resources, and by representing their efforts among the faculty and staff.

Second, there can be great value in affiliating or engaging with a larger organization or ministry. Many Christian efforts and communities struggle with being somewhat insulated from the surrounding culture. Partnering with a larger entity enhances support, resources, visibility and opportunities for the group. These are some of the services A Rocha USA, for instance, is striving to provide for its various community chapters. Being part of a larger family also comes with obligations, of course, and ideally adds a component of healthy accountability to one another in the movement.

The next step in mobilizing is assessment—taking stock of the cultural context, specific needs or issues, and available resources. Good assessments help startup groups target how to move forward in their communities. Here are three helpful questions new groups are asking:

1. How is our community impacting the planet now?

2. What could we be doing to better steward creation?

3. How do we get there?

The first two questions can be answered in a variety of ways. The easiest is simply to look around and talk to people in the know. Is there an efficient recycling system in place? How are we protecting and managing natural areas? How does our energy use break down? What can we learn from other communities that are doing a good job in some of these areas? What "best practices" do we already have in place?

This general approach is a good start and usually results in plenty of workable ideas. It's important to figure out what is already being done in your community, because there is little sense in reinventing the wheel or duplicating efforts. One of our pushes on Wheaton's campus was to introduce low-flow showerheads into some of the dorms. I got one installed in the bathroom on my floor, and some guys actually started to wait in line so they could use the single conservation-friendly shower. We found out later, though, that all the showers already had low-flow showerheads. I was about to feel really silly, but when we measured actual flow rates, we found that the new model actually saved more water than the others (0.75 gallons per minute more). Still, it was a close call.

Some communities are getting an even better picture and more rigorous data by performing full-fledged environmental audits that include energy, water, food, paper, waste, grounds keeping and transportation. Northland, A Church Distributed (Longwood, Florida) ran a comprehensive environmental audit on its new, sprawling facilities, which it has posted online, and is working now to implement the resulting recommendations.[2] The audit covered energy and water usage, solid waste generation, landscaping, purchasing policies and general operations. They even sorted a week's worth of trash into thirty-four categories to help uncover opportunities to reduce, reuse and recycle solid waste.

Calvin College (Michigan), Asbury College (Kentucky) and Palm Beach Atlantic University (Florida) are three of the many campuses that have also conducted energy audits. Berea College (Kentucky) even factors the amount of student travel to and from campus (spring break road-trips, flying home for Christmas, etc.) into their energy consumption totals.

This approach takes more expertise, research and participation from various departments within the community, but it is a great learning experience for all involved and provides a rigorous baseline from which to quantify future improvements.

Ignite. Once some foundations are laid, it can be helpful to step out from the quiet organizing phase to publicly ignite the movement. Many

Dispatch: Thad Salmon and Dustin Ford of Asbury College

Environmental stewardship has long been a topic of discussion at Asbury College. For years, special events have occurred sporadically, and several clubs have formed and then disbanded. In the spring of 2007, though, this conversation had a climate change. Matthew Sleeth (author of *Serve God, Save the Planet*) gave a chapel message that semester, and it inspired several students to find out more about the call to live simply and care for God's creation. These students formed a weekly discussion group with Nancy Sleeth and Andy Bathje, an administrator at the college. Both of us were blessed to be members of that group.

We spent the next few months reading Sleeth's book and working through ideas that would lead us to action. We organized cleanup events, during which we removed dozens of old tires and metal pipes from a creekbed near the school, and we hosted a creation care speaker. At the end of that semester, we decided that our small but faithful group would become the second student chapter of A Rocha USA.

In the fall, A Rocha Asbury became fully active. We were so excited to see our numbers triple at our first event of the school year! We have continued to meet regularly and have hosted a few campuswide events. While it's not always easy to find people who are willing to put real effort into the movement, we have been greatly blessed with encouragement from the Sleeth family and the administration of Asbury College. In fact, we recently submitted a proposal that led the college to include "Stewardship" alongside "Scripture, Holiness and Mission" in its four-part Quality Enhancement Plan, a project that will guide Asbury's goals in the coming years. This is a great step for creation care here, and hopefully, A Rocha Asbury will continue to contribute during this critical time.

groups aim big and work to attract attention in healthy and constructive ways. The greater the proportion of a campus, church or community engaged and inspired by the movement, the more effective that group tends to be in bringing change. Good launchings energize the team, attract others to participate and quickly build momentum for the cause.

One highly effective way of doing this is to hold a public forum and invite a compelling guest speaker in. This could be a chapel talk, evening lecture, sermon, panel discussion or any other platform that is already established as a legitimate forum in the community.

In the spring of 2007, Matthew Sleeth delivered a chapel talk at Asbury College and generated a buzz around creation care issues on a campus that had been mostly disengaged. A small creation care club of students and staff had been working to encourage recycling, but the very week after Matthew's talk, a much larger group of students showed up for a club meeting. The club soon became a student chapter of A Rocha.

Guang-Xi. With the grassroots effort underway, it's important to keep developing and deepening relationships.

Chinese culture understands that an integral key to making progress lies in Guang-Xi: the powerful network of relationships. The most important resource for any movement is its people and connections. Ours is fundamentally a relational task, and the bottom line is that both the problems and the opportunities we face are much better engaged when we do so together.

As the apostle Paul put it, we are all parts of the same body—the church—and we depend on one another to function in wholeness (see 1 Corinthians 12). God gives different talents, skills and responsibilities to each of us and has spread his work out across the whole church. He calls us to be in communion with him and with each other. There is great power when we work together for good.

Collaborative approaches are becoming more established across the creation care movement, and we're seeing the importance of developing relationships and networks across departments and disciplines. Forming and launching a grassroots movement within a community is highly valuable, but it is also just a beginning.

Many churches and campuses are forming creation care task forces that represent the various stakeholders and decision makers in their respective communities. The Environmental Stewardship Committee at Calvin College, revamped in 2002, now brings together faculty experts as well as representatives from the physical plant and administration to develop guidelines for sustainability and then implement them on campus. Other specific key players involved in similar task forces elsewhere include architects, librarians, resident life staff, finance staff and key student leaders.

Campuses with committees like this effectively in place include Eastern Mennonite University (Virginia), Messiah College (Pennsylvania), Goshen College (Indiana), Wheaton College (Illinois) and Abilene Christian University (Texas). Vineyard Boise and Northland, A Church Distributed, are two churches with strong creation care teams as well. Whether in a church or on a campus, these committees integrate sustainability questions into the very operational structure and cultural fabric of the institution. They provide communities with a critical locus for discussing relevant environmental issues and streamlining the path from discussion to decision to action.

Empower. If grassroots movements launch well, they can build up a strong pulse of momentum. Sustaining this valuable momentum requires having a follow-up plan, such as a hands-on project, that anyone can get involved in right away. This can range from continuing educational efforts through a book study or seminar to actually engaging in hands-on creation care, such as through a workday with the local park district. The longer the gap between the launch and follow-up, the more people will lose interest and drift off. The best idea is usually to integrate follow-up opportunities into the big event itself.

This is where the concept of low-hanging fruit is so critical—both in empowering the movement and in encouraging more people to get involved. Every young movement can use quick and quantifiable successes. Going for the low-hanging fruit first is not only more efficient, it also helps build confidence and an encouraging record of achievement.

Soon after its launch in 2007, the student chapter of A Rocha Canada at Trinity Western University (Langley, B.C.) partnered with its campus to build compost bins. Over the next four months, they composted about 715 pounds of waste from the college cafeteria. Group members also partnered with A Rocha Canada on field days, organized Earth Week events, hosted monthly fellowship dinners and conducted monthly road cleanups. All of the above efforts were meaningful, productive and—most importantly for a new group—realistically doable. In fact, their good efforts were recognized almost immediately when they surpassed nine other nominees to win the 2008 Environmental Hero Award sponsored by Langley's Member of Parliament Mark Warawa, parliamentary secretary to the minister of environment in Canada.

Starting with some low-hanging fruit, as the Trinity Western group did, is a good tactic. As time goes on, groups can build capacity to engage in more-involved projects.

This is what Earthkeepers, the student creation care group at Messiah College (Pennsylvania) is doing. In the spring of 2007, they successfully proposed planting a vegetable garden in the lawn by the science building. This very involved project took some planning and long-term commitment to sustain. The brilliance behind the garden is that it was planted in a very visible location and gave people an opportunity to engage in making a real difference with as much or as little time as they had to spare. All people had to do was stop by while walking back from class or lunch, roll up their sleeves and pitch in.

As former Earthkeepers President Lauren Kras explained to me when I visited, the intentional goal is to always provide meaningful ways in which their peers can plug into and feel empowered as part of the garden project, regardless of how much previous experience they have. After all, this was the first significant garden many of the organizers themselves had planted. Their efforts were rewarded when, within the first two weeks alone, they had seventy-five volunteers who put in an impressive total of more than two thousand volunteer hours. The project was such a success that the administration extended support for it, the campus cafeteria and some faculty members have bought shares for the produce, and Earthkeepers has since branched out to develop a composting system that will turn food waste on campus into compost for the garden.

Meanwhile, the Earthkeepers group at Wheaton College (unaffiliated to the Messiah group of the same name) partnered with A Rocha Wheaton to organize an energy-saving competition between campus housing units in March 2008. They worked with key staff members to standardize and track the different dorms and residences (in terms of square footage, number of residents and percentage of energy saved over the previous month) and held special events and creative artwork displays to foster dialogue about energy use and conservation.

There was a twist to it as well: aside from bragging rights and a polar bear sponsorship for the winner, all the money saved through using less energy would go to help dig water wells for a community in East Africa. The initiative earned positive traction throughout the student body, and many students got involved turning off lights and unplugging unused appliances. At the end of the month, the college measured the difference in energy consumption compared to previous records and found that the school had saved five thousand dollars—enough to dig an entire new well through Lifewater International.

Both of these above projects are good examples of student groups that were able to bring lots of different people together to get their hands dirty and make a difference. What started out as a mustard seed in each case has since germinated, shot up green growth, and is bearing good fruit.

Uplink: Janel Curry, Dean of Research, Calvin College, and Chair, Evangelical Environmental Network

Reflections on What We Have Learned

Recently at Calvin College we celebrated the tenth anniversary of the Calvin Environmental Assessment Program (CEAP).[3] Those of us who were at the first workshop, at which CEAP was conceived, were both amazed and thankful for its continuing success. However, upon reflection, we see that this program represents but the first step in our continuing journey toward caring for God's good earth.

The Calvin Environmental Assessment Program represents the initial stage of Creation Care, where we must first know ourselves. CEAP has involved faculty who dedicate regular lab sessions or course projects to collecting data that contribute to an overall assessment of Calvin's environment. We now have ten years of long-term data sets, which include everything from water quality in the various water bodies on campus as well as habitat and floristic diversity, to studies on food sources, to data on what it would take to become a carbon-neutral campus. Through this process, faculty and students have learned about themselves and their place on this particular piece of the earth. We have developed a *habit of knowing ourselves.*

At Calvin College, we learned early in the history of CEAP that knowing ourselves was not enough. Such knowledge needs to be integrated into the planning structures of the campus. In 2002, at the initiation of CEAP faculty, the structure and mandate of the major committee overseeing environmental concerns was changed to ensure that it represented the major environmental interest groups on campus, included those that had the information and data related to such issues, and also included important decision-makers. A committee that was once floundering has now moved forward, including the development of a statement on sustainability that has been accepted by the Board of Trustees. This committee has also been involved with further assessment of our "environmental state of the campus" to enhance our benchmark data to assess whether we are making progress. I consider all of these

structural initiatives as part of a process of *holding ourselves accountable.*

Holding ourselves accountable for how we use our particular piece of the earth is not enough. We live within larger communities and regions. Mapping our connection to the larger environmental community has also been crucial for Calvin College. To encourage less urban sprawl, reduce pressure for more parking (at the cost of green space) and thus reduce our carbon emissions, we have worked with the Grand Rapids transit system to encourage more bus ridership. But we have also expanded our thinking about the place of the physical setting of the campus to the larger ecosystem. I call all of these moves a process of *re-envisioning our "sense of place."*

One particular aspect of expanding our sense of place has been our focus on the Plaster Creek Watershed. Calvin College is on a divide between two watersheds, one of which is the Plaster Creek Watershed. Many of the college's planning decisions involve water runoff into the creek. The college has a great deal of interest in the watershed because 50 percent of the approximately seven hundred faculty and staff live within the watershed as do over 3,200 Calvin alumni. So part of our expansion in vision of our place is to incorporate the watershed in which we live into our framework.

Plaster Creek is a spawning ground for Lake Michigan salmon, and its corridor is the only place in Kent County where the state-threatened beak grass is known to grow. It is also the home to turkey, deer, red fox, muskrat, mink, crayfish, heron and trout. However, fish and macroinvertebrate communities are rated poor, and the water quality of the creek has declined to the point where there is a state-issued warning that its waters are not safe for even partial immersion. The levels of bacteria in Plaster Creek are among the highest of any stream in the Grand Rapids area, partially the results of its 106 storm water permits.

The watershed has increasingly become the focus of a variety of Calvin College grant proposals that integrate the college's classroom research, as well as its science education partnerships with local schools, with the needs of planning agencies attempting to address the environmental problems of the watershed. As part of this effort, Calvin College has become the home of the Plaster Creek Watershed Working Group, which has a website that has become the depository for data on Plaster Creek.[4] The college also has become a partner with the West Michigan Environmental Action Coalition and others in the community as they attempt to construct a watershed plan and develop action plans to restore the creek. Calvin College is seen as a key player because of the research of its faculty and students, but also because of its links to the churches within the watershed. The Classis Grand Rapids East of the Christian Reformed Church has many churches and members within the watershed and is one of the few institutions that bridges the social divides of the watershed, crossing socio-economic boundaries as well as political ones. The Plaster Creek Watershed is home to 40 percent (that is, 2,400 households) of the Christian Reformed Church households in the Grand Rapids area.

An institution's expanding sense of place needs partners. Calvin College's most recent move in creation care has been to link with others. The college is involved with both the Grand Rapids Community Sustainability Partnership and the Michigan Higher Education Partnership on Sustainability.[5] These learning communities challenge us to set yet higher goals, make us humble through their example and provide us with creative ideas in that process. They keep us from being complacent.

Throughout Calvin College's journey toward caring for the earth, we have deliberately drawn on our institution's particular multiple identities: a religious tradition that values "the creation" and a sense of "calling," a scholarly tradition that values research, an egalitarianism that values an effective faculty-run governance structure, a high valuing of teaching and involving students, a city that itself has a robust sustainability agenda and a long commitment to a broad liberal arts curriculum. A successful campus effort in creation care draws on the strengths of one's institutional and cultural identity.

8

Molehills
Overcoming Obstacles to Growth

We are too young to realize that certain things are impossible, so we'll do them anyway.

William Pitt to William Wilberforce, *Amazing Grace*

My parents frequently declare war on the moles in their garden. I happen to think moles are kinda cute, but they do kill the grass and make bothersome tunnels all over the lawn. If you want to be on good terms with my parents, I would discourage leaving little dirt mounds strewn around the yard. It is not a big deal, but it is a nuisance.

We have genuine obstacles to overcome in the creation care movement. While these obstacles may at first appear insurmountable, many can be overcome with some perseverance and imagination. Like the molehills in our yards, they can be a nuisance and a challenge but, as the old adage goes, we don't need to turn them into mountains.

Some of the barriers described below are a result of how we think about creation care (Molehills in the Mind), while others have to do more with how we practice creation care (Molehills in the Movement). Molehills in the mind are the most common objections or questions we face when talking about creation care; molehills in the movement are the most common obstacles I've seen groups facing. Both of these descriptive categories are connected with one another and have the potential to impede our progress toward good stewardship if they are not addressed.

Molehills in the Mind

Molehill 1: "The earth is going to burn up, so why should we worry about taking care of it?" We should take care of the earth now because God asks us to and he still cares very much about it. We do not know when the final judgment will come, but when Christ does come back, it would be far better if he finds us doing what he asked (see Lk 12:35-48).

On top of this, when the Bible talks about the earth being "laid bare" by fire (2 Pet 3:10), theologians clarify that the language it uses is referring to a refining fire—very much in the same way metal ore is put into the fire to burn off its impurities. In other words, the earth will be refined and renewed when Christ comes back, not destroyed. This is reminiscent of Noah's time, when God sent a flood to "destroy" the earth. In both cases God's purpose is to purge the earth of evil and renew his good creation.

This does not mean that, since God will finally renew the earth, we can abuse it now. Even though our bodies will be resurrected at the end, we are still careful to take care of our health in this life. So, should we take good care of the environment? John the apostle emphasizes this by warning that there will be a time for "destroying those who destroy the earth" (Rev 11:18). Alongside war, bad environmental stewardship is a primary way humans are currently destroying the earth.

Molehill 2: "Aren't people more important than animals?" Yes, people are more important than animals. But animals are important too, and the good news is that we usually do not have to choose between the two. Jesus teaches us that even though humans are more valuable than birds, God takes care of us both (see Mt 6:26). By caring for creation, we are ultimately caring for both humans and animals—treehuggers are peoplehuggers too. Besides, we can usually avoid coming to the point where someone has to choose between, let's say, eating the last panda or starving to death. A lot of bad decisions will have to be made before a sad situation like this occurs.

Molehill 3: "Aren't we forming 'unholy alliances' when we work with environmental groups?" We should be carefully eager about working with mainstream environmental groups. Just because an organization is not Christian does not mean it is anti-Christian. On the contrary, a lot of mainstream environmental groups have significant numbers of Christians on their staff and among their leadership. Jesus clearly calls us to be distinct from the world while also engaging within society as Christians. (We will revisit this more in chapter twelve, "We Hug Trees for Jesus.") We may face some criticism for this position, but we are in good company: Jesus himself was often criticized by the Pharisees for hanging out with "the wrong crowd."

Molehill 4: "Is conservation important even in places with plenty of resources?" When we are blessed with abundant resources, we should be grateful but not wasteful.[1] Christ says, "From everyone who has been given much, much will be demanded; and from the one who has been entrusted with much, much more will be asked" (Lk 12:48). Many of us in America have access to an abundance of resources that millions of our neighbors can only dream of, including simple things like clean water and three meals a day. This is both a blessing for us to enjoy and a challenge to steward creatively for the benefit of others.

Moreover, resources are usually not as abundant as we think they are. Most areas of the country (and world, for that matter) are under a lot of stress trying to keep up with growing demand. So much irrigation water is now pumped from the Colorado River that it often dries up before reaching the Gulf of California. Meanwhile, the vast eight-hundred-mile-long Ogallala Aquifer underneath the Great Plains is so overdrawn that it is losing twelve billion cubic meters a year and, at this rate, could dry up by the year 2050.[2]

On another front, new power plants are being constructed at alarming rates to try to keep up with growing energy demands across the United States. As a result, more fossil fuels are extracted, resulting in increased pollution, national security threats and pressure to open up key protected areas for drilling, such as the Arctic National Wildlife Refuge in Alaska.

Furthermore, obtaining, processing and distributing these natural resources is not free. All town and city water has to be treated, piped to individual residences and then filtered before being discharged. This results in a lot of costs and consumes large amounts of energy.

Molehill 5: "Isn't going 'green' more expensive and therefore bad stewardship of our money?" Not quite. It's true that living an environmentally friendly life—at least in the developed world—can sometimes cost more. Many "green" products such as natural cleaning supplies and hybrid cars are more expensive than some of their "nongreen" equivalents.

First, the bottom line here is not money; the bottom line is holiness. The gospel is not revenue neutral, and it will often cost us time, money or other resources to do the right thing (as discussed at the end of chapter three). God has called us to be good stewards of creation, and he gives us all the resources we need in order to follow his will. Two of these God-given resources are our time and money. So it makes sense that we would expect to use some of both in caring for creation. It is well worth paying the extra dollar for a bag of coffee that is shade grown and fair trade; the other product is cheaper largely because it is grown unsustainably using underpaid and abused laborers in Third World countries.

Second, we can do a lot of things that will not cost any extra and may even save money. Buying and consuming less is the obvious all-around winner here. In terms of diet choices, cutting back on meat and eating more vegetables, grains and vegetarian protein sources, such as tofu or lentils, is ultimately cheaper, healthier and better for the earth.

Compact fluorescent bulbs may cost significantly more to purchase, but use around 75 percent less energy and last up to ten times longer than incandescent bulbs—for a total energy savings of up to thirty dollars per bulb.[3] This works on a larger scale too: the 26,000-member Prestonwood Baptist Church in Plano, Texas, won an award from the Environmental Protection Agency in 2007 for adopting energy-conservation practices that saved one million dollars over the previous year's utilities bill. This is money that can now be used for missions and other vital church ministries.

We care for creation because it is the right thing to do, and if we do it creatively, we often save money.

Molehills in the Movement

Molehill 6: The C word. C stands for commitment. And it can be an issue. Commitment is not something we do well in this culture. A quick glance at church membership trends and national divorce rates demonstrates this point. In contrast, we serve a God who values commitment; who patiently worked with the Israelites over many generations, showing great faithfulness as time and again they prostituted themselves to foreign idols; who is so committed to us that he sent his very Son to die for our sins rather than give us up for lost. Commitment matters to God.

But, for a myriad of reasons, commitment does not always seem to matter enough to us. The narcissistic culture we live in has so permeated our value systems that we will happily commit to something (or someone) for as long as we find it fun or rewarding. Once the good feelings fade, often we do too. Or workloads pick up as the year progresses, or a romantic interest sparks and relegates everything else to the background.

It is no secret that volunteer movements—whether in churches, communities or campuses—often struggle from a lack of commitment among many of their members. One exception to this commitment problem is in sports teams. Playing competitive sports is demanding, exhausting, uncomfortable and stressful, and it is a wonder that anyone would care so much or work so hard to row a boat faster or throw a ball farther. Yet making a spot on the team can be quite competitive. And if you slack off, you risk getting cut. We can learn some valuable lessons from this example.

When recruiting for a group, it helps to be upfront and transparent about what participation or membership entails. Caring for creation should be fun, but like most things worthwhile, it involves work too. It may help to have some initial buy-in, such as a modest membership fee or a jointly written covenant so that members are on the same page about what group expectations are. Of course, everyone should be given opportunities to participate when they are available, even if they can't make a full membership commitment. The standards can be set loosely, but they should also be maintained. Otherwise, it is likely that the group will struggle to accomplish significant, lasting service to the community.

This may sound harsh, but movements ranging from campus chapters to community groups to membership-based organizations have found commitment instrumental in focusing their efforts. When I was involved in a creation care campus group as a freshman, our list had well over twenty members, but only a fraction of these came to meetings. This number slowly dwindled until it was down to two students and our faculty adviser. I suppose you could say we were in the "ebbing" stage back then. It was a frustrating and demoralizing time, and for a while I thought we were just going to fold for the year.

Instead, we adapted our approach and gave one last push. First, we realized that people join a creation care movement because they want to practice creation care, not just talk about it. This can be intimidating, but the first practical project certainly doesn't need to be Herculean in nature, like securing administration funds to install solar panels for all the roofs on campus. Try something more modest and low-hanging, such as participating in a creek cleanup or recruiting a professor to lead a bird-watching trip. Everyone needs to get the hang of walking before they can run, and baby steps are nothing to frown upon.

In time, we developed practical projects, such as a long-term partnership with the local forest preserve district to help study their wetlands and monitor amphibian biodiversity. We also did some grassroots publicity by giving short talks in many of the big science classes, which attracted new members who were eager to get involved and help bring change.

While it was important to the members that we could depend on each other, we also did not want to leave out classmates who were interested but unable to commit at the same level. So we devised a three-layer system of belonging: board members, regular (but still highly valued) members and friends. Friends were included on our e-mail list and invited to participate in any activities but could not actually hold office, lead a project or vote. So far it has worked well.

Molehill 7: Taking leadership seriously. Many motivations lead people to assume leadership roles. Some are very noble but others are more self-serving. Even when we sincerely try, it can be hard to discern what our true motivations are.

Leadership can appear attractive because of the power and prestige that goes along with it. The title of "President," "Director" or "Chairperson" just seems to have a nice ring to it. Jesus teaches, however, that leaders are called primarily to serve and to sacrifice for the people they lead—not the other way around. The greatest leader on earth bent over to wash the dirty feet of his followers and calls all aspiring leaders to do the same.

Those who assume roles of responsibility for the wrong reasons will be disappointed when any perceived glamour fades and the hard work picks up. They will either realign their motives and grow more fully into their roles or lose interest and drift away. This is one reason it is important to be prayerful and discerning when either choosing leaders or accepting a position. As a mentor once taught me, leadership should be presented as a function and service, not merely as a title or position. In other words, we act out our leadership.

Sometimes, forming leadership teams where all members hold equal say can help build accountability and mitigate some of the pitfalls of having hierarchical positions such as a president, vice president and business manager. This is what the Justice Matters Club at Dordt College (Iowa) has found useful.

The Justice Matters Club is a student group that advocates for social and environmental concerns at Dordt. In the past, they struggled with club officers who were attracted to positions of leadership but did not pull their weight after being elected. Now the group functions around a much more open and flat structure: anyone who shows up to planning meetings can be part of the leadership circle, and they vote on three peers to serve on equal footing as stewards of the treasury, of communication and of meetings. They try to be clear that these roles imply different categories of service, not a hierarchy. For instance, stewards merely help coordinate the group; all decisions are made by consensus.

Molehill 8: Scientists vs. treehuggers. Grace College (Indiana) is a small Christian school taking big steps toward caring for its local environment. Much of this is thanks to its president, Ronald Manahan, who also teaches creation care theology at the Au Sable Institute. He helped lead efforts to transform an asbestos-contaminated wasteland on campus into a healthy marsh and to begin a water-quality initiative in local lakes and rivers staffed by the college through a 250,000-dollar external grant. On this campus, the administration seems surprisingly far ahead of most of the student body in prioritizing environmental stewardship.

Fostering Eden—the A Rocha student chapter at Grace—is the exception. Although the group got started only in 2007, they wasted little time in working with the administration to engage their classmates by planning events like a creation care chapel. They also invited me and Ryan (one of my roommates) to their 2008 Earth Week celebration, where we had a great time fellowshiping with their small but lively group.

However, one of the concerns they voiced to me over a midnight coffee run was that few people from the sciences had gotten involved in their group. They felt unsuccessful in engaging a large proportion of the campus community, particularly those who should have special reason to care, given their studies in the life sciences. They wondered if the science community on campus viewed them as "liberal treehugger activists" and so avoided associating too closely together.

Their observation is a common one. A single community often contains different groups who are concerned about environmental stewardship. One group contains those with a science background or academic interest in the field. Enter the self-proclaimed "nerds" with their microscopes, field guides and waders. This includes science faculty or majors on a college campus and practicing scientists in a church or community.

Another commonly occurring group tends to be turned off by highly technical science and is mostly enthused about activism and grassroots organizing. This crowd sometimes resembles the stereotypical "treehugger" or "granola" and is infamous for organizing events like no-shower week and for wearing clothes made from organic hemp.

This is a broad, but often reasonably accurate, generalization. While there is considerable overlap, these two groups tend to have their own unique atmosphere, goals and preferred methods of working for change. On one hand, science is crucial because we need to recognize and understand how creation works if we are going to take care of it. On the other hand, activism, especially when endowed with passion and creativity, is vital to an effective and energized movement. We need each other, and there is beauty in the diversity we bring together.

A holistic creation care movement is not about scientists *versus* treehuggers (or any other generalized category we can think of), it's about scientists *and* treehuggers working together. In reality, though, one group usually dominates the other. This can be hard to overcome and takes time, flexibility and intentionality. Fostering Eden is off to a good start because they realize that this is one of their weaknesses. They are intentionally trying to change this and to develop relationships with the science department. For one, their adviser is a biology professor.

Molehill 9: Overcoming inertia. The law of inertia states that unless opposing energy is applied to the system, an object in motion stays in motion and an object at rest stays at rest. I once accidentally drove off the road in my grandmother's car. Thanks to inertia, it jumped the curb and the right wheels climbed up a tree trunk, throwing the car off balance and flipping it upside down. It finally rested on its hood, in inertia, and could not be made to move again until a tow truck dragged it away.

Social inertia has been one of the biggest obstacles facing the creation care movement in general. Some liken our task to turning a battleship with a canoe paddle. It can be painfully slow.

Communities of any size usually have a very entrenched culture that can be hard to impact. Public opinion toward creation care may be shifting quickly in our favor, but usually it takes lots of patience to build enough momentum for widespread change. Do not be discouraged if you can't seem to make progress in your community for a long time. We get to do the good work God has prepared for us and then trust him with the results. The good news, once things finally do get moving, is that inertia works both ways; now the movement will be that much harder to derail.

Sometimes, however, we do everything to our very best ability, all the right steps are in place, and there is still little progress. In cases like this, it may just be about the timing. Keep trying, and ask for counsel from community leaders such as pastors or professors who have a good feel for the current culture.

However, it may take time before the conditions are ripe enough to continue. There comes a point when it is okay to step back for the moment and regroup. This isn't giving up; it's just being patient. I was recently contacted by a biology student at MidAmerica Nazarene University (Olathe, Kansas) who came to this conclusion after struggling to get a recycling club going on campus. There seemed to be interest from some of his classmates at the beginning of the year, but it was not sustained for long. The group effectively folded for a semester, but the student is planning to try again to "get some life back into" the recycling movement there.

Molehill 10: The credibility hurdle. The apostle Paul wrote to his trainee, Timothy, "Don't let anyone look down on you because you are young, but set an example for the believers in speech, in life, in love, in faith and in purity" (1 Tim 4:12). Building credibility as a young person in a sea of elders with years of experience or advanced degrees can be tough, to say the least.

This is something I face often. In many of my meetings, e-mail exchanges and conference calls, I am the youngest and least experienced person in the group by between ten and forty years. Yes, it can be intimidating.

Though my generation is relatively new on the scene, we still have a lot to offer. We bring idealism and energy to the picture, which God delights in and can use to accomplish good beyond our levels of education and experience. Though some of the people I interact with in the creation care movement are initially surprised by how young I am, the vast majority of leaders today are eager to work alongside and mentor me. They realize, as we should too, that the time is fast approaching when my generation will be taking on more leadership responsibilities in the church, and they are eager to help prepare us for this.

Paul continues by instructing Timothy to set an example for the believers "in speech, in life, in love, in faith and in purity." Our work is cut out for us. Whether they are faculty members, administrators or pastors, we are careful not to take the openness of our senior leaders to working with us for granted. Credibility must still be earned slowly and can be damaged in a careless instant.

We should strive to be exemplary in how we carry ourselves, how we interact with others and how we engage issues. This may not come naturally to us, so good preparation is key. For a while, I was under the foolish impression that, when it came to public speaking and presentations, I could just get up and wing it. Sometimes this worked fine. Other times, however, my lack of preparation was glaringly obvious. After a couple of meetings that I blundered my way through, one of my professors sat me down and gently but bluntly advised me that I needed to work on my preparation. It was good advice; careful preparation is key to building credibility.

Full Speed Ahead

As we move forward in the creation care movement, we often face challenges. I have tried to list some of the common obstacles that I've found while organizing, but my list is not exhaustive. Whenever we are doing God's will (even many times when we aren't), it is no surprise that obstacles or opposition come up. Together we can understand these challenges for what they are, make the appropriate adjustments and move on.

> Therefore, since we are surrounded by such a great cloud of witnesses, let us throw off everything that hinders and the sin that so easily entangles, and let us run with perseverance the race marked out for us. Let us fix our eyes on Jesus, the author and perfecter of our faith, who for the joy set before him endured the cross, scorning its shame, and sat down at the right hand of the throne of God. (Heb 12:1-2)

Uplink: Ed Johnson, President, Au Sable Institute of Environmental Studies

As the former president of a Christian college, Sterling College (Kansas), I witnessed first-hand in marvelous ways the power of the Holy Spirit in the passion of college students who understand they are called to serve Christ and his people around the world. From a perspective of thirty years in higher-education administration, I have never seen a greater opportunity to change the world for Christ than through the current creation care movement on our nation's college and university campuses. The scientific evidence is clear and the scales are coming off our eyes. Global climate disruption has once again reminded us that we are the Lord's earthkeepers. The current student movement is providing energy and hope to environmental and justice issues that will be catastrophic, particularly for those living in the Two-Thirds, developing world. It is less a new way of seeing, although it is that, than it is a new way of serving. Not just serving a brother or sister but the very planet itself.

If we are to heal the planet, Christian students must significantly multiply their servant leadership roles in the creation care movement. For it is not enough to say that environmental stewardship issues are among the most critical moral and ethical issues of our time, and in fact, in human history. For you, these issues go far beyond that: they are spiritual issues that go to the heart of who we are and whose we are. For every visible molehill we see as air, water and species degradation, we understand the real molehill is profound: Given the clear evidence of our misuse of his creation, how now shall we live?

It is imperative that the commitment and energy of today's and tomorrow's students move beyond passion to the coordinated, scalable, sustained actions that will answer that profound question. Many of you have been given the gifts and will be called to the new frontier of social entrepreneurship: changing the world through leadership in nonprofit organizations that never lose sight of mission (saving lives or changing lives) while operating under the business principles that will ensure maximum impact through effective stewardship of resources. Many of you will be called to encourage your colleges or universities to sign the American College and University Presidents Climate Commitment and thus join hundreds of other institutions in moving toward climate neutrality. Others will be instrumental in local community environmental stewardship projects. Each of us is now called to change our personal behaviors, our family life and our vocational impact, and our communities in different ways and at different times.

The bottom line is that you and I can't sit this one out. I challenge you to read the parable of the good Samaritan with new eyes: it is the earth that is lying at the side of the road. We all put it there, and we have the opportunity and the commandment to help it heal. In this redemptive moment, God is counting on you!

9

Sustaining Sustainability
Keeping the Movement Alive

"I wish the ring had never come to me. I wish none of this had happened."
"So do all who live to see such times, but that is not for them to decide. All we
have to decide is what to do with the time that is given us."
A conversation between Frodo and Gandalf, *The Fellowship of the Ring*

And the winners of the divine election to rule over all creation are . . . us.

We did not have to campaign for this position; it is an honor that God gives to us who share his image. As in the Spiderman principle, however, with great privilege comes great responsibilities. Our superiority over the created order means that we must exercise good stewardship in looking after it. This commitment is not something we can afford to disregard or burn out on.

Persevering over the long run is no simple task, however, especially given the challenges in the world today. To sustain our commitment to God for creation will require that we grasp the wisdom of sustainability and practice the discipline of community.

The Wisdom of Sustainability

In 1983 the United Nations convened the World Commission on Environment and Development to address growing concerns that rapid economic and social development was depleting our natural resource base and causing wide-scale environmental degradation. The landmark report they published in 1987 was formally titled "Our Common Future" but is often simply referred to as the Brundtland Report, after former Norwegian Prime Minister Gro Brundtland, who led the commission.

One of the major contributions of the Bruntland Report is that it defined the concept of sustainable development as "development that meets the needs of the present without compromising the ability of future generations to meet their own needs."[1]

While the concept of sustainability is trendy now, it is really just a recent articulation of an age-old concept that runs right through both creation and the Bible: God created the world to have limits. Sustainability comes from maintaining a balance within these limits.

Gravity is a limiting force that keeps us (and everything else) from literally falling off the face of the planet. The physical-chemical nature of water makes it less dense from 0 degrees to 4 degrees Celsius so that ice floats and lakes do not freeze from the bottom up. In wisdom, God has given his creation limits from the very beginning, as he reminded Job: "Who shut up the sea behind doors when it burst forth from the womb, when I made the clouds its garment and wrapped it in thick darkness, when I fixed limits for it and set its doors and bars in place, when I said, 'This far you may come and no farther; here is where your proud waves halt'?" (Job 38:8-11). It's easy to take these things for granted, but God-ordained limits are what bring order out of the chaos in the world.

God also created healthy limits for humans and the environment to flourish within. We can work only so hard and so long before we need to eat and sleep. Similarly, the land can produce only so much harvest before it too needs to rest and be replenished with nutrients. This is one reason God instituted the Sabbath and modeled it for us when he made the world:

> Remember the Sabbath day by keeping it holy. Six days you shall labor and do all your work, but the seventh day is a Sabbath to the Lord your God. On it you shall not do any work, neither you, nor your son or daughter, nor your manservant or maidservant, nor your animals, nor the alien within your gates. For in six days the Lord made the heavens and the earth, the sea, and all that is in them, but he rested on the seventh day. Therefore the Lord blessed the Sabbath day and made it holy. (Ex 20:8-11)

And then later for the land:

> When you enter the land I am going to give you, the land itself must observe a Sabbath to the Lord. For six years sow your fields,

and for six years prune your vineyards and gather their crops. But in the seventh year the land is to have a sabbath rest, a sabbath to the Lord. (Lev 25:2-4)

These boundaries are not merely suggested guidelines; they are moral imperatives. Remembering the Sabbath is one of the Ten Commandments.

God blessed the Sabbath and made it holy (see Gen 2:3). By respecting the limits of sustainability, we worship God and honor the way he has created us and the rest of the world to function; ignoring them is counter-productive and even destructive.

This is evident in environmental crises: when we do not practice sustainable fishing, we start to run out of fish; when we do not control our use of energy, the excess greenhouse gases we release throw atmospheric cycles off balance and cause the climate to change. This is also evident in our personal lives. Our departure from sustainability is a cultural and personal struggle fueled by a drive to be more productive and more successful. How many of us consistently take a weekly day of rest when we do not try to accomplish worldly ends or get ahead on responsibilities? What about if we include not checking e-mail on our rest day?

Sustainability is a practice sorely worth making a priority today. Taking time to rest while surrounded by the demands of work and life is crucial if we are not going to burn out.

But it is more than just for our health and sanity. Committing to times of rest is also an acknowledgment that we are not ultimately in control— God is—and that our abilities and strivings are not what give us abundantly full lives—God does. It is an invitation to experience contentment in the provision of our Creator and to refocus our hearts and minds on his abiding love.

Overachievers for Christ?

So, what does this mean for our efforts to care for creation?

Spearheading a movement—or even just being involved in one—can be a consuming affair. How can we pace ourselves so that we avoid burning out? If we are advocating for the sustainable use of our planet and natural resources, how can we also ensure that our lifestyles and movement are sustainable too?

One important step is to be purposeful instead of simply driven. Having lots of drive and passion is an asset, but these qualities need to be channeled toward a clear vision and the right goals. If they aren't, we will end up expending lots of energy paddling in circles rather than making forward progress. Evaluating ideas and efforts against the group's vision can help focus our energy and streamline our efforts.

For instance, all groups hold meetings. But this is not why they exist. Rather, holding meetings is a means to achieve a practical end, such as building community, raising awareness about composting or planning a hiking trip. This practical end in turn serves the group's underlying mission, which could be expressed as something like "worshiping God by caring for his creation."

The environmental scene is awash with issues, initiatives, requests and proposals. Having a clearly defined sense of mission, goals and objectives will help determine how we prioritize our resources and what projects we take on.

Floresta and Lifewater International are two exceptional Christian organizations. Floresta is dedicated to poverty alleviation through sustainable agriculture and reforestation, while Lifewater International focuses on developing water resources in Third World settings. Both of these ministries are active in the creation care movement, but each has a clearly defined mission that guides what it chooses to do: one of Floresta's main activities is to plant trees alongside local communities, while Lifewater primarily drills water wells. Although teaching Christian students to care for creation is something they both value, this is not their mission and so is not among their primary activities. Gladly, it is the focus of another organization, Creation Care Studies Program, which runs semester-long study-abroad programs in New Zealand and Belize for college students.

Being purposeful can help narrow our focus, but at the same time it is possible to become too specialized. Most groups start with one main project or practical activity but quickly branch out into related needs as they grow in capacity. This helps prevent the problem of tunnel vision—when we focus in so specifically that we lose sight of the bigger picture—and also keeps all our eggs from being in one basket. This way, if the main project or partnership concludes or falls apart, there are other active efforts to keep things going.

Advocates for a Sustainable Future (ASF) is a student club at Gordon College (Massachusetts) that officially started in 2007.[2] They aimed big and started an organic community garden on campus as their major project. The garden was a big success, and in the fall they were even able to raise money by selling the harvest of herbs and vegetables at a farm stand on campus.

Not to be pessimistic, but a lot could have gone wrong with the garden. Pests could have invaded the plants, thoughtless pranks could have ruined the harvest, or the college could have decided to use the space for other purposes in following years. An organic garden can be a rewarding but sometimes unstable project.

But the garden is not the only activity ASF got involved in. They also found time and energy in between weeding to start composting in a couple of dorms (which also supports the garden), contribute relevant articles to the school paper, support campus recycling efforts and hold awareness events ranging from a creation care chapel talk to an exuberant outdoor harvest celebration. By diversifying into these various activities, the members of ASF were able to maintain their focus without unnecessarily boxing themselves in.

Of course, the ultimate focus we all share in this is God. He is the ruling priority in our lives: "Remain in me and I will remain in you. No branch can bear fruit by itself; it must remain in the vine. Neither can you bear fruit unless you remain in me" (Jn 15:4). This is not a groundbreaking idea, perhaps, but nonetheless one that is awfully hard to practice consistently.

The Discipline of Community

Keeping our priorities straight is one reason we need community. Maintaining our focus and priorities is very challenging. On our own, it would be impossible, but in community we can find mutual accountability and support.

Having accountability helps us stay on track, especially those of us who sometimes lack the self-discipline to stay purposeful instead of merely busy. Being in community means we can spot when we get off track in the first place. This is why organizations have a board of directors, churches have elders, colleges have trustees, and many individuals are part of small groups.

On top of accountability, a healthy community provides much-needed support. There is an interesting phenomenon in aquatic biology where the size of a fish can be affected by the amount of space it has to grow into. For instance, largemouth bass can grow to upwards of fifteen pounds (the record of 22 pounds, 4 ounces, was set in Georgia in 1932), but if put in a twenty-gallon fish tank, they have trouble growing even to a pound.

Likewise, the size of a movement can be affected by the amount of room it has to grow into. This can be the actual size of the larger community (campus or church), but it can also refer to the capacity of its leaders. If one person is trying to micromanage everything, then "everything" will likely get only as big as that one person can control. On the other hand, if a capable team works together to delegate and share the burden, the capacity can grow exponentially without any one person needing to overwork.

While delegation is critical to the sustainability of a movement, mutual respect and trust in the group is critical for it to work well. Building this level of trust takes time and intentionality. The ideal picture is a safe community where each member is highly valued and where there is also vulnerability and space to utilize and challenge each other's strengths and weaknesses.

Jesus fostered such a community among his disciples, and then he delegated to them and us the task of proclaiming the gospel through the power of his Spirit. He certainly does not need our help to accomplish his will, but if he chooses to work through us as his church, we can likewise risk sharing our work with one another.

Another supporting aspect of community is that it breeds new leaders to help carry the movement into the future. Continually mentoring new leaders is critical to sustaining a movement. This is an especially urgent issue on campuses, where regular membership turnover is guaranteed and ranks as one of the most effective movement killers. Four years pass in a flash, and without fresh leaders to carry on the mantle, campus groups can quickly lose momentum and fade out of institutional memory. Movements stay vibrant and effective by constantly recruiting new participants and developing new leaders.

Building an Epic Community

Fostering healthy community is an intentional and never-ending process.

On a trip to South Florida, Matthew Sleeth and I were invited to a special creation care awareness and outreach event called Epic-Earthcare. Epic-Earthcare was organized by Epic-Remix, a young, emergent-type church that meets in a school auditorium on Sunday evenings. They went all out for this event and involved a bunch of relevant community groups in a mini-expo set up in the auditorium. Tables held displays for causes ranging from eco-friendly house supplies and fair-trade clothing to green building and local activist groups.

What made Epic-Earthcare so impressive was that it was well organized and smoothly delegated to an energized team of dependable volunteers according to their gifts and talents. Some folks were in charge of food and refreshments; others handled setup and coordinated with the displaying organizations; yet others put together publicity materials and an introductory film for the evening. As a result of their effective publicity, a solid crowd showed up, enjoyed plenty of good food and had a great time learning and fellowshiping together.

It was very inspiring to see how well the organizing team got along and sincerely enjoyed working together. Part of how they had developed such a strong community became evident later that evening, when the team reconvened at the pastor's home to hang out and celebrate the successful event. Spurred on by lively conversations and tasty snacks, the impromptu gathering ran way past midnight before winding down.

I assumed that this "after-party" was a unique occurrence, but was surprised to find out that it happened almost every week after the church service. Over time and through such intentional efforts, they had developed a strong community with one another that enabled them to make Epic-Earthcare look like a cinch to organize.

Energy Dependence

Ultimately, though, our combined energy is still not enough to sustain us in a world with so many pressing problems and overwhelming demands. Even when we respect boundaries, take Sabbath rests and support each other in community, there will be times when life is overwhelming and it's easy to feel we have nothing left to give. But there is great hope in Paul's boast that "I can do everything through him who gives me strength" (Phil 4:13).

True sustainability is honest and humble enough to realize that, in order to do God's work in God's way, we need nothing less than God's strength. He is the eternally renewable energy source that we depend on. And we can live and rest in peace with full assurance that God promises to sustain us so we can keep on doing his will.

> Do you not know? Have you not heard? The LORD is the everlasting God, the Creator of the ends of the earth. He will not grow tired or weary, and his understanding no one can fathom. He gives strength to the weary and increases the power of the weak. Even youths grow tired and weary, and young men stumble and fall; but those who hope in the LORD will renew their strength. They will soar on wings like eagles; they will run and not grow weary, they will walk and not be faint. (Is 40:28-31)

Uplink: Jeff Greenberg, Professor of Geology, Wheaton College

It is my honor and joy to contribute something to complement the insights of my brother Ben. He writes and lives as an embodiment of what sustainability means to me.

For almost thirty years I have taught with attention to mentor young people gifted by God as agents of reconciliation. As believers in Jesus, we are called to reconcile all things to the Lord. Romans 8:19-21 describes our potential as nothing less than Christ's power manifest in fixing what has been so long broken. Today I believe that this ridiculous vision can be fulfilled through us. Evidence exists in the new band of disciples taking up the challenge. Sustainability in ministry is cast for us in 2 Timothy 2:2, as those who receive the Spirit's fire pass it along to the next cadre of the faithful, then to be continually entrusted to succeeding generations of apprentices. Readers of this book, take the words inside and get in line. Do your kingdom service with an eye for who can come alongside to learn from you.

Sustainability is a direction defined for us via the two "books of God," in the Word written as Scripture and in the works created everywhere as nature. Good theology reinforced by good science emphasizes that we must be at work sustaining what the Lord has ordained. That which is not sustained dies. On the level of an individual life, death is inevitable. At the level of entire species or earth systems, the loss likely involves the magnified undoing of many other lives and functions. Unfortunately, we of the affluent societies typically fail to recognize the functional limits of earth in providing for our costly lifestyles.

Equilibrium as concept should be seen as one of the "fingerprints of God" in sustainable systems. In a 2005 article, I attempted to describe the genius behind both the human body's systems and those that maintain (sustain) the grand-factory status of planet Earth.[3] In each case it is essential to study and understand the limits of functional conditions.

Economic greed and scientific ignorance exist together in subversion of righteous decisions required by our informed faith.

In 2005 three Wheaton College geology students spent two months in South Africa to work with an Afrikaans Youth With A Mission (YWAM) staff member. The students served a project to map out the extent of domestic waste influxes from the permanent and transient (squatter) settlements in Pellsrus Township. The project's ultimate goal was to identify problems and to offer and even implement some solutions.

The township area is located next to the rather affluent community of Jeffreys Bay, known for its outstanding surfing and shelling beach. Wastes traveling through the township by way of ditches and ravines end up along the beachfront and contaminate the coastal waters. Rudi, the YWAMer, proposed the study of this problem for his master's of environmental management thesis. With the students' help and my counsel, geotechnical maps were made, water samples were analyzed, composting "ecosan" toilets were constructed and tested by township residents, and two types of small-scale gardens were established for exhibit. The integrated study and development projects were facilitated in part by local pastors and teachers. The desire was to see the initial accomplishments multiplied by community residents as they came to recognize benefits.

At the end of the two-month tour of duty, there was optimism about the effort. All the pieces necessary for sustainability appeared to be in place.[4] Today, my other friends at the Jeffreys Bay YWAM base tell me that with Rudi's departure, zeal to sustain the sanitation program also left. This is not to say that the YWAMers and locals don't care; it is just that they were already involved in other important work and did not possess the expertise to steward the environmental concerns of the region. Rudi's local position was not sustainable.

The amount of actual money applied to the Pellrus project was tiny in comparison to even smaller projects done by large organizations. The mostly voluntary contribution of time and expertise in this case contrasts greatly with more professional jobs. Well-funded professionals could probably never equal both the quantity and quality of accomplishments made over those two months. Neither a humbler nor a better-funded and staffed attempt at community transformation could survive long without enduring local ownership.

An important lesson for all of us, writing or reading this, is that sustainability needs people. In our context, these people are believers in Jesus. He alone gives us the motivation to go and do with greater regard for others than ourselves. He alone instills the Holy Spirit as our guide. The harvest is indeed ripe, but still two-thousand-plus years later, the laborers are too few. The Timothy 2:2 principle of reproducing ourselves in ministry is something we must do better.

I have great hopes for my students to become fruitful workers. I pray that some of them will acquire the mantel of leadership with the godly insight of modern prophets. The fields of creation we call the environment and the fruits of God's provision we call resources need you.

Part 3

A Bigger Vision

10

Synthesis
Connecting into the Bigger Picture

We cannot solve the challenges of our time unless we solve them together.
Barack Obama, 2008

I woke up shivering in my sleeping bag. It was starting to get light outside, and I could hear Peter Illyn from Restoring Eden moving around the kitchen tent, trying to start the stove. Next to me, Don Bosch—an A Rocha member and creation care blogger—started stirring in his bag. "What time is it?" I asked.

"Seven," he replied. "Time to get going."

Wriggling out of my bag and into a cold, stiff pair of jeans, I grabbed my toothbrush and stumbled out of the tent. I looked around. On most camping trips I would be surrounded by trees or on the banks of a remote river. This time, however, I was with a group of college students and hardy adults in an open field behind the Vineyard Boise church. We were there for the second annual creation care conference that the church's Let's Tend the Garden ministry was organizing. Camping on the church grounds was a nice way to cut down on housing and transportation costs.

As we saw in chapter six, under the leadership of Pastor Tri Robinson, the Vineyard Boise church has been very active in creation care issues since 2005. The purpose of its annual conference is to spread awareness and provide in-depth education about various aspects of creation care. To do this, the church brings together leaders from various national creation care organizations to teach seminars and workshops, which are open to anyone who wants to come and learn about good stewardship.

On the East coast, Northland, A Church Distributed, is also working to reach out to churches. In the winter of 2008, their environmental ministry, Creation, I Care, organized C3—a conference set on their central Florida campus but geared to a national audience. Though similar to the conference at Vineyard Boise, it lasted one day and was specifically targeted toward equipping pastors to lead their congregations in creation care.

Besides being a wonderful time of fellowship with friends in the creation care movement, the conference provided good opportunities for me to meet new colleagues and learn more about what their various ministries are up to. Sometimes I find it easy to get so focused on my own efforts and immediate surroundings that I forget we are working within a much broader context.

There is a lot of good work going on in the creation care movement. New initiatives and leaders are streaming onboard as part of a building wave of active concern. These developments are encouraging, but we still have plenty of work to do together.

The Nehemiah Principle

Our task is analogous to what the prophet Nehemiah faced when trying to rebuild the city wall around Jerusalem. The entire wall lay in ruins, with all the gates burned down; rebuilding would be a mammoth task. On top of this, there was stiff opposition from nearby kings, who plotted to keep the Israelites from becoming a strong nation again.

Nehemiah knew he could not do this on his own. So he brought all the remaining families together and commissioned each of them to tackle the part of the wall they were closest to. He also armed them and set some of the men as guards to discourage attacks from the surrounding kings. By doing all this, Nehemiah took a mission that seemed impossible and divvied it up among the whole community so that each group had a manageable task. Then, by coordinating all the groups with one another, he ensured that, piece by piece, the wall was successfully rebuilt.

As in Nehemiah's time, we have a vast mission on our hands today. Many communities and ministries are engaged in creation care throughout the United States and the world. They serve diligently alongside us, even though we may sometimes feel isolated while building up our part of the movement. Just as the Israelites were able to combine their many efforts to rebuild the Jerusalem wall, so may we also join to build up the creation care movement.

For anyone coming fresh onto the scene, however, it can easily be overwhelming trying to search out and understand all the different ongoing projects. And those already involved need help to coordinate individual efforts so we can work together more effectively and efficiently.

This networking role used to be filled by the Christian Environmental Council—a broad group of leaders and activists who would meet annually to renew relationships and collaborate on projects together. The Christian Environmental Council is no longer active, but the conferences at the Vineyard Boise and Northland, a Church Distributed, are providing a semi-regular locus for everyone to meet up for fellowship and teaching.

For their part, the Au Sable Institute of Environmental Studies faithfully brings together Christian students for training in the science of stewardship every summer and winter on multiple campuses. In the summer of 2008, the Au Sable Institute also partnered with the Evangelical Environmental Network to host the first in a series of creation care consultations among senior leaders and organizational heads. The purpose of these daylong events is to explore common goals and find ways to connect all our individual pieces into the larger picture.

One of the key pieces here is the role of students in the broader creation care movement. Various groups have been engaging students in their outreach efforts for some time, and now the nascent steps of a student movement are finally gaining momentum. One of the more recent sparks that helped get things going was the Wheaton Summit in 2007.

The Wheaton Summit

Early in my senior year at Wheaton, I had the opportunity to visit Houghton College's Star Lake campus in Adirondacks State Park. Houghton College (New York) owns this wonderful retreat facility on the shores of the lake, which it uses to run a semester-long environmental studies program for college students.

By this point, I had been working in the creation care effort on Wheaton's campus for three years. Our efforts to green the campus and community were finally starting to bear visible fruit, which in turn attracted outside attention. Soon peers from other campuses were asking questions about what we were doing. We heard encouraging reports of similar initiatives at other schools, such as a LEED-certified building project at Judson College (Illinois) and an award-winning recycling program at Point Loma University (California).

On this particular trip to Star Lake, I got to interact with students from Houghton and a couple of other Christian colleges. They were very interested in helping to green their campuses, but were looking for ideas and support to go about it.

As we chatted into the night by the crackling fire, we realized that if all of us were struggling to make progress on our own campuses, there were probably similar groups on other Christian campuses facing the same issues. It would be very helpful to find a way that we could connect more with each other to learn, brainstorm and fellowship together. This vision developed into plans to organize a multiday student summit at Wheaton to coincide with an upcoming visit by Sir John Houghton.

Back at Wheaton, I floated this idea past the A Rocha Wheaton team and contacts in the faculty and staff. Remarkably, everyone I talked to responded enthusiastically, and momentum started to build. Nine classmates and I formed a planning team and quickly got cracking in the two months we had left, three weeks of which fell over Christmas break.

Organizing the summit was a tremendous amount of work. And it was often intimidating, because no one on our team had experience organizing an event of this kind and magnitude. Moreover, there were no other student creation care summits that we could learn from or base our hopes on and expectations off of. We were, in many ways, trying something fresh—and it was anyone's guess how it would turn out.

But the summit seemed like a good and timely idea. So we kept moving forward, and in late January of 2007, about eighty representatives from fifteen colleges and another fifteen organizations converged on Wheaton's campus. Students and faculty came from Gordon College, Eastern University, Dordt College, John Brown University, Messiah College, Azuza Pacific University and Trinity Western University in Canada, among others. Staff and leaders representing groups such as the Evangelical Environmental Network, the United Nations Foundation and the National Wildlife Federation participated in sessions.

The three summit days passed in a whirlwind of people, events, ideas and discussions. There were so many friends to make and so much talking to do that our meetings could have lasted much longer.

A group photo from the Wheaton Summit. Photo by Annabelle Ng.

We heard from various senior leaders, such as Jim Ball, Susan Emmerich and Paul Corts. Sir John spoke in several venues as well, engaging us with both his scientific expertise and his Christian faith. He shared from his experience leading the Intergovernmental Panel on Climate Change scientific working group for more than ten years and opened up for questions and answers. He was frank with us that global climate change is an immense problem only expected to get worse. He also shared a hopeful vision that we can still make a big difference if we are willing to practice the Christian values of sacrifice and sharing.

Beyond the formal agenda, we were also intentional about building community through worshiping, praying and breaking bread together.

We invested time and effort into developing relationships and connecting with each other and, in the end, we had the beginnings of a modest community.

Some of the summit participants returned inspired to develop new initiatives on their respective campuses. Gordon College got their student creation care organization going and Messiah worked on bringing together their various campus groups with environmental interests. About a year later I found out that two participants who first met while at the summit were getting married. Apparently we didn't just build community—we doubled as a matchmaking service.

Tipping Points

The Wheaton Summit was an inspiring time of fellowship, yet we were reminded of just how much room there still is for growth.

About fifty non-Wheaton students came out for the summit—the rest were speakers and organizational representatives. This was a fine showing, but we had originally planned for 100-150 students. Given the number of Christian campuses alone, and how many invitations we sent out, it's somewhat surprising that more students did not respond.

The mediocre attendance at the Wheaton Summit was also consistently reflected in other events, however, such as the conferences at Vineyard Boise and Northland, A Church Distributed. Even though they too recruited heavily on a national level, far fewer participants came out than they originally hoped and budgeted for.

We talk a lot in the creation care movement about having finally reached a tipping point in the church; progress was slow for many years, and now things are finally taking off. So it is somewhat perplexing that we are not attracting larger crowds at these conferences. Have we really reached a tipping point then? Our experiences on the ground just don't seem to be lining up with this claim.

Some of the confusion here comes about because there is more than one so-called tipping point to aim for. It's quite clear that we have reached a tipping point in *awareness*—many Christians would affirm that serious environmental concerns exist and are important for the church to address. At the same time, however, it appears that we have not yet reached a tipping point in *action*. This is the next benchmark we are striving toward. While ongoing education should be a priority, our main focus will increasingly become to empower the church from a position of awareness and concern to a position of action and advocacy. To make progress toward this next step, I think we will need to prioritize two things in particular: nurturing a grassroots student movement, and developing greater symbiosis among everyone on the creation care front.

A Student Movement

There are hopeful signs that a new student creation care network called Renewal is finally taking off.

Over the 2007-2008 academic year a core group of students and recent graduates came together to develop a proposal and recruit campuses and senior advisers; twelve of us met together outside of St. Paul, Minnesota, for a planning retreat right before classes began in August 2008.

The retreat was a resounding success, and we left with a clear sense of our shared mission—"To inspire and equip the student generation to lead its communities with justice and compassion in Christ-centered stewardship of all God's creation." This retreat also led to a student leaders' training summit hosted by Eastern University, in October 2008, where Renewal was formally launched as a functional and active network.

The stakes are high here. A student network is difficult to sustain over the long run, because of the turnover as students graduate and also because students tend to have relatively tight financial resources. However, a lot of productive collaboration can happen, even if the network starts out small.

Movements in the past—such as with civil rights and the Vietnam War—were guided by the wisdom of elders but largely propelled by the passion and idealism of young people who were outraged by the injustices in society and were audacious enough to believe that a better world was within reach. When it comes to caring for creation, the church today needs a powerful burst of energy to get out of the pews and onto the proverbial plow. And I believe that devoted students and youth are one of our best hopes to make this happen.

More Symbiosis

A student movement on its own will not be enough. We also need to explore ways that all of us working on creation care can more intentionally support and partner with one another. Developing strong collaborative efforts and healthy relational networks will strengthen the movement and build the crucial elements of trust and mutuality that lead to biblical cooperation in a competitive world. This is important because competition within the movement can sap a lot of momentum and be a big obstacle to effective mobilization.

Competition can occur at all levels between individuals, churches, campuses and organizations. It is a curse because it separates us and pits us against each other instead of bringing everyone together. It is also unnecessary. We have so much urgent work to do and not nearly enough people doing it that there is little justification for Christians to choose a path of competition over cooperation; we need all the help we can get.

In ecology, we call cooperation that is mutually beneficial "symbiosis." Symbiosis occurs when two different species share a similar niche and have a better chance at survival if they work together. It happens all the time in nature, and it occurs because each species has strengths that the other benefits from.

Consider the Yellow Watchman goby and the blind shrimp. Both marine critters share the same burrow. The shrimp is much better at digging burrows than the goby, but it is blind and so very vulnerable to hungry predators. The goby was never created to be a digger, but has great eyesight: it can even swivel its eyes independently.

So they join forces. While the shrimp digs their home, the goby keeps watch. The shrimp keeps one antenna touching the tail of the goby so that as soon as danger approaches, both critters dash into the burrow for safety. It's a partnership that makes good sense.

This sort of collaboration is starting to happen more intentionally in the creation care movement today. For instance, Care of Creation and

A Rocha USA separately started working to mobilize churches in the United States. Both organizations also have active groups in the United Kingdom and Kenya already working closely with each other. So it makes good sense for these two organizations to partner at some level in the States, and this is exactly what's happening. Led by Ed Brown, Care of Creation is setting up creation care seminars in churches based on his book, *Our Father's World*. A Rocha USA cosponsors these events and explores ways for folks to follow up on what they learn by getting involved in hands-on conservation projects. A Rocha USA also supports the teaching ministry of our former executive director Matthew Sleeth, mobilizing our members to host speaking engagements and help coordinate travel logistics where possible. Both of these partnerships have been mutually meaningful and fruitful.

So I say, "Bring on the symbiosis!" We are often more effective working together than alone. And even if we do not have a lot to offer each other, there is plenty of room in the creation care niche for many people and groups to work alongside each other. As Jesus said, those who are not against us are for us (see Mk 9:40).

It is a big creation, there is a lot to do, and time is running out. We need each other like the blind shrimp needs the goby. Not very romantic perhaps, but true.

Uplink: Dorothy Boorse, Professor of Biology, Gordon College

Standing on the Backs of Giants

O God, enlarge within us the sense of fellowship with all living things, even our brothers the animals, to whom thou gavest the earth as their home in common with us. We remember with shame that in the past we have exercised the high dominion of man with ruthless cruelty so that the voice of the earth, which should have gone up to thee in song, has been a groan of pain. May we realize that they live, not for us alone, but for themselves and for thee, and that they love the sweetness of life.
St. Basil the Great, Bishop of Caesarea (329-379)

The current American Christian environmental movement comes out of a long tradition in Christianity of environmental stewardship. St Francis of Assisi is probably the most well-known proponent of environmental care in the early church. However, many other people believed in living very simply and caring for nonhuman creation. These included Celtic Christians and church fathers like St. Basil the Great.

Many years later, the modern American environmental movement arose because of growing awareness of human impacts on our world. Many Christians were not connected to the environmental ethic in their own historic traditions. In response, Christian scholars of the latter twentieth century rose to the challenge of finding and expressing the Christian basis for creation care. This scholarship led to the establishment of a number of centers for study and institutions for action. One of these was the Au Sable Institute of Environmental Studies, a Christian college field station, founded in 1979 from the Au Sable Trails Camp for Youth. Au Sable faculty has put its stamp on a generation of current environmental care faculty across the United States. Another is the Evangelical Environmental Network, founded in 1993 to promote ethical use of the environment among evangelicals. Now there are far too many groups and institutions to mention.

Scholars like Cal DeWitt, Loren Wilkinson, Susan Power Bratton and Stephen Bouma-Prediger set the stage for several decades, training a generation of Christians who are now faculty and church leaders. Today's college students benefit from years of quiet effort by the generations prior who set up institutions, wrote books and spoke the truth to power. The youth ready to put their backs into the work today are standing on the backs of these faithful believers, who held out a vision to tend and keep the garden and will, in turn, give a hand up to children unborn, who will care fifty years from now.

11

Red, Blue or Green?
The Role of Politics in Caring for Creation

This is not a Red State issue or a Blue State issue or a green issue. It's a spiritual issue.

Richard Cizik, 2006

"Who did you vote for in the last presidential election?" I was caught by surprise with this bold question from the well-known reporter. Directly behind her the network camera was focused and ready to record my answer. Not quite sure how to respond, I replied: "I don't think answering your question will be helpful here." And we moved on to other topics.[1]

I was being interviewed for my work on environmental issues, but the real story was how evangelicals like me are starting to recover a broader social agenda, and the implications this shift will have on our political positions.

A Hot Topic

"Evangelical Voters Leaving Republican Flock"

"Evangelicals Go Green—Will Conservative Candidates Follow Suit?"

Headlines like the ones above—both from ABC News—are becoming more common these days. It's a widely held understanding that evangelicals vote their values—and that this practice is not about to change. What does appear to be changing, however, are some of the values that evangelicals hold to. And this perceived shift has been the subject of intense media speculation.

There is no surprise here. Self-proclaimed evangelicals make up almost a quarter of the nation's voters. And being evangelical at the turn of the millennium meant, for most people, voting along the Republican ticket. The Republican Party tends to be strongly pro-life, and their presidential candidate in 2000 and 2004, George W. Bush, made a big deal about being a born-again, evangelical Christian himself. These were two key factors that led leaders of the religious right, such as Focus on the Family's James Dobson, to enthusiastically endorse Bush both times. Many evangelical Christian voters followed suit on Election Day, squeaking him into power in 2000 and then keeping him there with an impressive 78 percent of their vote in 2004.

But times appear to be changing. Some polls suggest that fewer evangelicals are now voting along either party line; no party fully represents our values any more. It used to be that we took a stand on a few key issues such as abortion, gay marriage and teaching evolution in schools. However, this is changing. Our earlier convictions are still important, but we have come to realize there are many other moral issues we should also care about. The church is recovering biblical concerns such as caring for the environment, advocating for immigrants, fighting poverty and more. And that puts us simultaneously at odds and in favor of policies within both major parties. It appears that we are not so easily co-opted any longer. This worries the Republicans, encourages the Democrats, excites the press and causes conflict in the pews.

Beyond Partisan Politics

Politics is one of the more divisive issues in our church and culture. And it has a large impact on how Christians—evangelicals in particular—view caring for the environment. There is an unfortunate and unnecessary association between the environmental movement and the so-called radical left that espouses teachings such as the Gaia Hypothesis (where the earth itself is viewed as a great, big, living organism) and promotes practices such as population control through abortion.

If there is truth to the assertion that "liberals" have hijacked environmentalism, it is only because the so-called conservatives ditched it years ago in favor of supporting big industry. In reality, though, being "green" is not a liberal-conservative or Republican-Democrat or red-blue issue—it's a moral and spiritual one. We are all human and we are all called by God to be good stewards; responsibility for the environment belongs to all of us. Our common concern for this planet may have political implications, but it is inherently nonpartisan and urgently needs to go beyond partisan politics.

There are encouraging signs that this is happening. People who are polar opposites on the political spectrum have begun sounding the alarm and working together on the issue of climate change. Pat Robertson and Al Sharpton are jointly featured in a series of advertisements about climate concerns. Al Gore is not the only one to have recently published about environmental issues; Newt Gingrich put out a book in 2007 titled *A Contract with the Earth*.[2] In the 2008 election campaign, both Barack Obama and John McCain were eager to address climate change and offered strong environmental positions and records. Within the first month of winning the election, then-President-elect Obama was quick to commit his administration to making serious global-warming legislation a priority.

We are moving in the right direction, toward cooperation and collaboration on common ground. This is good news because politics has the power to make a big difference when thoughtfully exercised in the interest of protecting creation.

The Power of Politics

When it comes to uniting to make a difference in the world, one of the most obvious ways to do that is through our votes. Voting is a powerful right that citizens in a democratic society can exercise to make a broader impact than they would be able to leverage on their own. Closely related to voting is the practice of lobbying our elected officials—expressing our opinions to the leaders and lawmakers that are supposed to represent us in the government.

The stakes are high. On one hand, a good law can bring sweeping benefits on many levels that far surpass individual efforts on the ground. On the other hand, a bad law can override years of meaningful progress.

Of course, there is a lot of fine print. No law is perfect—the endangered species act has made a big difference in conserving biodiversity over the years, but it has weaknesses that opponents regularly pounce on. The Kyoto Protocol is a well-known example of an international agreement that is limited and flawed, but which almost all participating countries (with the notable exception of the United States) have seen enough value in to ratify. The sad reality is that there are often so many competing interests that it takes a significant amount of compromise to pass a robust piece of legislation.

Once a law passes, it still has to be enforced in order to be effective. Enforcement takes funding, but it also takes political will, which can be a problem. Mountain-top removal coal mining should not be legal in Appalachia because it violates the Clean Water Act by inadvertently burying or contaminating hundreds of miles of streams, wetlands and underground aquifers. But coal companies have more resources and better access to decision makers than local communities do, so the practice of mountain-top removal continues to spread.

This touches on another, more sinister, power involved in politics, a corrupting power that exerts itself on politicians, lobbyists and leaders: the hunger for greater influence, status and fame. Time and again we have witnessed leaders become so caught up with themselves that they trade noble service and good intentions for the pursuit of unholy extravagances, sinful indiscretions and idolatrous self-promotion. We can probably all think of examples where this has happened.

Just because there is significant risk involved, however, that does not imply we should avoid engaging in politics. The church has largely avoided engaging in environmental stewardship for so long out of the perceived risk that it could have a liberalizing effect on us; and we now see that was a mistake. After all, there is much biblical precedent for political involvement. Prophets and leaders like Moses were empowered by God to lobby their leaders and protest to their kings. It often ended poorly for them (Moses' hard-fought success seems to be more the exception), but it was nonetheless a calling from God that the prophets were obedient to. God even places some of his followers in influential positions within pagan kingdoms: Joseph in Egypt, Esther in Persia, and Daniel in Babylon are three notable examples.

So given the inherent risks involved, how can Christians engage in politics with integrity?

Daniel as a Model

I have found the book of Daniel especially helpful here, especially as it has to do with living in the context of a pagan empire. Daniel and three friends—Shadrach, Meshach and Abednego—were brought to Babylon after Judah was conquered and employed in the king's service. They quickly rose in stature within the Babylonian government, and Daniel served as a trusted adviser in two administrations (Kings Nebuchadnezzar and Belshazzar). Daniel and his friends were not simply victims of the empire any more—Daniel had become one of its highest ranking officials! But through it all, they maintained a clear focus on God and an unwavering commitment to pursuing righteousness. They all stuck their necks out to avoid eating meat that had been offered to idols. Later, Daniel's friends were thrown into a blazing furnace for refusing to worship an idol of the king. Daniel was not spared either—in a separate famous incident he was thrown into a den of lions for praying to God.

In all three trials, however, God rewarded their faithfulness by delivering them and increasing their favor in the eyes of the kings. But even so, their commitment to God was independent of whether he chose to spare them from suffering. Right before Shadrach, Meshach and Abednego were thrown into the furnace, they affirmed:

> O Nebuchadnezzar, we do not need to defend ourselves before you in this matter. If we are thrown into the blazing furnace, the God we serve is able to save us from it, and he will rescue us from your hand, O king. But even if he does not, we want you to know, O king, that we will not serve your gods or worship the image of gold you have set up. (Dan 3:16-18)

The point of these stories is not that God rescued his followers (though that is certainly a nice bonus) but that he chose to use them to accomplish his purposes in a pagan empire, and was repeatedly glorified when they proved faithful and refused to compromise.

Those of us who aspire to directly engage our political systems, whether through protesting, lobbying or by running for office, can learn lessons from the example of Daniel and his friends. We can eagerly serve

God within the empire, but we are still to be set apart from it. Our highest commitment remains with God, and there can be no compromising when it comes to truth and righteousness. It will take a lot of courage to stand firm and be ready to sacrifice when necessary, but we can find strength through Christian community and constant prayer.

It is far more important to find favor with God than with this often-fickle and perverted world.

Contemporary Promise

Engaging in politics may be challenging, but there are good success stories and current initiatives in the creation-care movement that we can turn to for inspiration and opportunities.

Whenever the Endangered Species Act (ESA) has come under attack, Christians have been quick to step in and coordinate a response. In 1996 a number of denominations rallied together to help thwart attempts by Congress to weaken the ESA. They sent in letters of protest, met with their elected officials and ran nationwide advertisements drawing parallels between the ESA and Noah's Ark. A group of evangelicals led by Cal DeWitt even held a news conference in Washington, D.C., where they brought a full-grown panther on stage. After the news conference, the group also met with then Interior Secretary Bruce Babbitt and House Speaker Newt Gingrich.

Most observers expected the ESA to lose out in the Republican-controlled congress, but the modified legislation did not pass in the end. Christians—and evangelicals in particular—had played a big role in this surprise victory. Years later when the ESA came under threat again, a coalition of Christian and Jewish groups called the Noah Alliance was formed to renew opposition against weakening the act.

One of the key members in the Noah Alliance is a Christian environmental organization called Restoring Eden. Aside from being part of the alliance, Restoring Eden also coordinates occasional lobbying trips with Christian college students in D.C. Their trip in the spring of 2008 was in collaboration with Christians for the Mountains to protest the practice of mountain-top removal in Appalachia. These efforts and others, such as the Evangelical Climate Initiative and Evangelical Youth Climate Initiative (see chapter four), are valuable components of a holistic Christian approach to caring for creation in today's society.

In addition to the focused campaigns by groups such as Restoring Eden, Christians also have a sustained presence in national policy discussions through the efforts of the National Association of Evangelicals and the National Council of Churches. Both groups actively lobby politicians on environmental legislation and put out newsletters to help their members stay updated. They also help put together letter-writing initiatives and other strategic opportunities in order to mobilize their constituencies when an important vote is approaching.

Their work is crucial. But whether or not each of us is called to directly engage the political sphere on creation-care issues, we all still have an important role to play in the politics of creation care because we, together, are the people. And it is the people who ultimately hold the political will in our society. Our leaders in the state capitals and in Washington, D.C., will rarely take bold steps forward unless they sense our collective support.

So our job is to help them feel the heat. We can do that by writing letters and calling their offices with specific concerns, and by taking to the streets when necessary and staging peaceful gatherings to get their attention. But, first and foremost, we will get them to act when they see that we embody our message in the way we live; that we are willing to vote with our pocketbooks and time schedules as much as with our voices and ballots; that we are holding ourselves to the same standard that we are asking them to set. When we start to change, they will get the message and follow suit:

> Great social transformations—the end of slavery, the women's and civil rights movements, the end of colonial rule, the birth of environmentalism—all began with public awareness and engagement. Our political leaders followed rather than led. It was scientists, engineers, church-goers and young people who truly led the way.[3]

We now need to lead the way.

Uplink: Jonathan Merritt, National Spokesperson, Southern Baptist Environment and Climate Initiative

Red, Blue and Green

Being a Christian and being a Democrat are mutually exclusive. At least that is the impression I got growing up in the Republican-red Bible belt where evangelical pastors readily coopted their pulpits to rail against Democrats and endorse Republicans by name. On any given Sunday walking into a church, it would not be abnormal to be greeted with both a handshake and a voter's guide.

It makes one wonder about the 36 percent of regular churchgoers who voted for Al Gore in 2000 or 35 percent who voted for John Kerry in 2004.[4] Or, the majority of younger evangelicals who responded "Barack Obama," when asked by *Relevant Magazine* in 2007 which presidential candidate Jesus would vote for.[5] Are these Christ-followers not welcome in our pews without the promise of partisan pulpiteering?

I am a lifelong conservative who is more red than blue in any light, but even I understand that this ought not be. Luckily, many in rising generations agree. We think that the church has become too political. We remain solid supporters of biblical values like the sanctity of life, but we have expanded our political interests to include historically progressive issues like global poverty, human rights and the aggressive care of God's creation.

As Ben Lowe wrote earlier, "that puts us simultaneously at odds and in favor of policies within both major parties." Rather than red or blue, we tend to be a little bit purple. As a result, we have become nomads, political orphans who care more about living a life consistent with the teachings and ministry of Jesus Christ than toeing a particular party line.

In a recent network news interview, I was asked which party I felt compelled to support as an outspoken Christian. I said, "That's the wrong question." The reporter was bewildered and asked for clarification. I responded, "As a Christian, I am not required to support a particular party. A better question is to ask, 'which *values* am I compelled to support?'"

You may remember that Jesus came to the earth in a time when Israel was dealing with its own partisan unrest. Yet he sided neither with the oppressive Roman government nor with the Jewish politicians striving for independence. Maybe Jesus knew that when people begin placing great faith in political parties, they may easily lose focus on him, the ultimate answer to our world's greatest problems. If Jesus were among us today, I am not convinced that he would claim either party. Instead, he would be the ultimate values-voter—one who would offer support on biblical issues no matter which party claimed the moral high-ground first.

As rising generations exhibit a greater amount of partisan diversity, let us not be divided over our party of choice. We must never attenuate our opposition to moral evils and injustice, but we should unite with others when possible around the values that we share. Finding common ground on moral issues like environmental stewardship will go a long way toward perpetuating the revolution we so badly need.

12

We Hug Trees for Jesus
Engaging the World for Christ

Although the stewardship we offer is intended to bring benefit to God's creation, the offering itself is one that we direct toward Almighty God, the Creator of heaven and earth, and Jesus Christ, his only Son, our Lord.

Fred Van Dyke, Address to the Wheaton Summit, 2007

Weaving through Philadelphia city traffic, we made a left turn and found ourselves on Potter Street. John Humphreys—an active member of A Rocha—and I had come to take photos of some dirt.

Of course, it was no ordinary dirt; this was fertile soil that would soon provide the foundation and nutrients for a lush garden of vegetables, herbs and flowers. We wanted to take some "before" snapshots of the urban garden project that The Simple Way and A Rocha USA were working on at the Potter Street Community.[1] The idea was to take a set of "after" photos later in the summer to compare and contrast the difference between a bare city lot filled with dirt and one that is alive with healthy green plants.

The Potter Street Community garden, along with another plot nearby, jointly make up one of three urban gardening pilot projects in the United States that A Rocha USA is helping to facilitate thanks to a generous external grant. The other two are in partnership with the A Rocha community group in Santa Barbara, California, and with Communality, a missional group living and serving in the poorest neighborhoods of Lexington, Kentucky. All three projects, while immediately focused on organic gardening, are just as much about helping urban neighborhoods reconnect with creation while putting fresh produce on their tables.

The main garden space is an open lot next to the Potter Street Community building, where the city recently tore down a condemned house. In the resulting narrow space, they have built a clever network of raised beds with distinct plots that different community members can take stewardship of. On the roof they have additional planters made from creative materials such as used truck tires and—my favorite—an old toilet.

As we chatted with members of the community about their vision for the garden, I was deeply moved by how much this project points to Jesus Christ and the gospel he preached. Through his life, death and resurrection, Christ came to redeem us from our sins and to offer us new life with him in a new kingdom and creation. What better way to illustrate this gospel than by cultivating a vibrant and fruitful garden on a previously lifeless and garbage-filled lot?

The Whole Gospel

The motto of the highly significant Lausanne Covenant of 1974 declares our Christian mission to be "the whole church taking the whole gospel to the whole world."[2] This calling must be kept front and center in our efforts to care for the planet. Our creation care movement today has a strong biblical and theological foundation, but it also needs to be integrally connected to the gospel.

Creation care is inherently a gospel issue because the environment is one of the ways we learn about God: "For since the creation of the world God's invisible qualities—his eternal power and divine nature—have been clearly seen, being understood from what has been made, so that men are without excuse" (Rom 1:20). This idea that creation is a witness to God is also found in Psalm 19:

> The heavens declare the glory of God; the skies proclaim the work of his hands. Day after day they pour forth speech; night after night they display knowledge. There is no speech or language where their voice is not heard. Their voice goes out into all the earth, their words to the ends of the world. (vv. 1-4)

These verses led the Reformation leader Martin Luther to declare, "God writes the gospel, not in the Bible alone, but also on trees, and in the flowers and clouds and stars."[3]

If we take this assertion—that God is partly revealed through his creation—to its logical conclusion, then when we degrade and destroy God's creation, we run the risk of diminishing his witness. Some Christians have likened it to tearing pages out of the Bible.

Of course, the flip side is also true. When we care for creation, we are adding to God's witness in the world. In the case of the urban gardening projects, the little green space they create in the middle of a concrete jungle is the closest that many of their neighbors may get to God's creation (and to their food supply).

Clearly, though, creation itself can't present a full understanding of the gospel. We may learn about many of God's attributes through observing what he has made, but we have no way of knowing that Jesus Christ came to the earth, died for our sins, rose from the dead and will come again in judgment. This is why we also have the Bible.

Reactions to the Gospel

History shows, however, that it is easy to focus too much on one aspect of the gospel and downplay the fuller picture. In the recent past, evangelicals have emphasized verbal evangelism and personal salvation, often to the exclusion of social concern and justice. This is in part a reaction against the social gospel, which took hold of many mainline Protestant churches in the late nineteenth and early twentieth century. Step by step, however, evangelicals are reengaging vigorously in the current issues of our society.

These developments are largely being welcomed by the world. Everyone likes it when Christians feed hungry people, dig water wells, provide emergency disaster relief or set up homeless shelters. But much of this goodwill disappears when we start to talk about Jesus Christ. Though the biblical gospel is all-inclusive in its scope and invitation, it is also necessarily all-exclusive in its demands: Christ is the only one able to die for our sins; we understand from the Bible that there is no other way to be saved except through him.

As a result, there can be a strong temptation to leave out some verbal parts of the gospel—especially the message of personal repentance and salvation through Jesus Christ alone—and instead witness only through acts of love and justice. This is sometimes described as evangelism by deeds instead of by words. This is a false dichotomy, however, and one we must be vigilant against.

This gospel—announcing the good news of the kingdom of God—includes both a restored society and restored citizens; it calls for repentance, salvation and renewal both on a societal level and on a personal level.

We cannot choose between words or deeds, just as we cannot choose between the Great Commission to go baptize disciples of Christ (see Mt 28:18-20) and the two greatest commandments to love God and our neighbors (see Mt 22:37-39). They are both integral parts of the same gospel, and we must wholeheartedly pursue them together. This may not be popular today, but Christians have never been called to popularity anyway.

Christ himself warns us that we can expect to face persecution and hardship if we stand for him—just as he did. Christ also promises, however, that if we do stand for him, he will stand with us: "And surely I am with you always, to the very end of the age" (Mt 28:20).

All About Jesus

It is important that we only move forward in the presence and power of Christ.

In chapter one, we looked at Colossians 1:15-20 as a basis for understanding that God is reconciling all things back to his shalom and that he is doing it through Jesus Christ. While the reconciliation of all things is extremely important, it is not the main point of this passage. Rather, the focus of this text is the supremacy of Jesus Christ in all things:

> He is the image of the invisible God, the firstborn over all creation. For by him all things were created . . . by him and for him. He is before all things, and in him all things hold together. And he is the head of the body, the church; he is the beginning and the firstborn from among the dead, so that in everything he might have the supremacy. For God was pleased to have all his fullness dwell in

him, and through him to reconcile to himself all things, whether
things on earth or things in heaven, by making peace through his
blood, shed on the cross. (Col 1:15-20)

Paul, the author of Colossians, leaves no ambiguity here. Our lives
and work are grounded in the ultimate reality of Christ and his mission.
This planet and everything in it belongs to him. We and all our efforts
belong to him. He is the bringer of shalom, and we are colaborers in his
mission.

This makes our motivations straightforward: we do it for Jesus. We are
working to bring the fulfillment of Christ's kingdom to earth, and so our
primary and ultimate focus must be on him. Everything else pales in
comparison—Christ is our all in all.

There is inexplicable joy in this reality. Mother Teresa taught that joy
is the mystery of love. She explained that when we are in love with Jesus,
we experience great joy in him, even as we are surrounded by setbacks
and suffering. She, of all people, should know.

This truth has been important to me in my efforts advocating for
God's creation. Even though the tide is changing in our favor, mobilizing
the church to care for creation continues to be an uphill struggle with a
good share of obstacles and opposition along the way.

My friends at the Evangelical Environmental Network (EEN)
experienced some of this pushback at a prominent evangelical
convention in 2008. They applied and were originally enthusiastically
accepted by the organizing staff to host a creation care display at the
convention. Later, however, they received a rushed notification from the
executive committee, informing them that they had reversed the staff
decision: the EEN would no longer be permitted to display at their large
gathering of evangelicals. No specific reason was given.

Incidents like this from within parts of the church—along with a
chronic lack of funding, occasionally sticky internal politics and a
painful awareness of the very real suffering of those who live in degraded
environments—make it easy to become exasperated and weary in this
effort. But we can find consistent strength and joy in the reality that we
are doing Christ's work, and we are ultimately doing it for him.

The greatest commandment calls us to love God with all our heart, soul, mind and strength. If Jesus Christ is our first love, we will experience increasing joy the more we grow in our devotion to him. This joy is unshakeable because its foundation is set in the Rock of ages and not in the ever-changing circumstances around us. When Christians work to care for the earth and nurture life, we can do so joyfully because our stewardship is about more than the created order—it's about the Creator himself.

Redemptive Relationships

As we move forward, we will also increasingly engage with people and entities that do not share our faith in Christ. We find this when interacting in the mainstream environmental movement, but we also find this simply from being in the world.

When others see the joy we have in Christ and the lives of holiness and sacrifice that we eagerly pursue, they will wonder what the basis for our seemingly strange behavior is. The answer is something we must be eager to share, but we must also not always wait for people to search us out first. Instead, Christ sends us out—he calls us to go and to take the initiative in bringing his good news to the world.

The world today knows it is in trouble and is looking for our help. Here are open doors to engage the world with the truth that is found only in Christ. E. O. Wilson, the preeminent Harvard biologist, Pulitzer Prize–winning author and outspoken secular humanist, wrote a book in 2006 titled *The Creation* in which he appealed to Christians for help in saving the planet. Secular scientists and leaders, many who used to be openly antagonistic toward Christians, are increasingly eager to partner with the church in addressing issues like climate change and biodiversity loss. This is a welcome development and presents promising opportunities to form redemptive relationships with others and to share openly about why we care for the earth and our neighbors.

Consider the Sierra Club, the oldest and largest grassroots environmental organization in the United States. Traditionally, the church has viewed the Sierra Club with distrust and, in return, the club has tended to view the church with disdain. Today, things are starting to look very different. As early as 1998, the club's executive director, Carl Pope, acknowledged in a speech before Ecumenical Patriarch Bartholomew I of the Greek Orthodox Church that

> the environmental movement for the past quarter of a century has made no more profound error than to misunderstand the mission of religion and the churches in preserving the creation. . . . We [his generation of environmentalists] sought to transform society, but ignored the fact that when Americans want to express something wiser and better than they are as individuals, by and large they gather to pray. We acted as if we could save life on earth without the same institutions through which we save ourselves.[4]

More recently, the Sierra Club surveyed its members and found that 47 percent regularly attend religious services of some sort.[5] The club also has developed an active faith outreach through its environmental partnerships office that has accomplished a lot of good work with Christians by supporting efforts to raise awareness on mountaintop removal, providing travel scholarships for creation care conferences, partnering with author Brian McLaren on his *Everything Must Change* book tour, and publishing a report titled "Faith in Action," which surveyed fifty faith-based environmental projects—one from each state in the Union.

Power Shift 2007

Through outreach efforts at A Rocha USA, I often had the opportunity to interact with people and initiatives that were far removed from my Christian faith. In November 2007, six thousand young folks descended on Washington, D.C., for the first national youth summit to address global warming. The mood was charged; an intense passion for change burned impatiently throughout the crowd. Organized by student leaders from the Energy Action Coalition and a host of other sponsors, Power Shift 2007 was an impressive feat of organizational skill and a testimony to how serious this rising generation is about fighting climate change.

The events lasted from Friday night through Sunday morning and culminated in a nonpartisan lobby day on Monday, where participants testified before a hearing of the Select Committee on Energy Independence and Global Warming. They represented all fifty states while lobbying House and Senate offices and then rallied in front of the Capitol Building.

I was asked by the organizers to attend and give three workshops of my choice to help add an evangelical voice to the gathering. The workshops I presented were all well attended by both Christians and non-Christians, and included a presentation of the biblical basis for environmental stewardship, an overview of how Christians are engaging in creation care and an exploration of what makes Christians unique and vital in the climate movement. The last workshop packed out the room and went a half-hour longer than scheduled in informal group discussions.

Being at Power Shift 2007 and interacting with everyone was both invigorating and overwhelming. I could agree with a lot of what was said and promoted there, but there were also significant aspects that I disagreed with. When in such settings, it can be hard to figure out if and how we should respond to such challenges. I struggled to walk the fine line of being honest and open about what I believe to be true without being unnecessarily offensive.

Still, I found the overall openness to engage with Christians and the Bible heartening. We may not always get open doors like this to point people to Christ, but when they do occur, they are well worth seizing. The crux of the matter is this: I was invited to go to a national, secular environmental gathering as a Christian to share my faith and read from the Bible; I got to go talk about Jesus with my peers, the majority of whom rarely hear his name anymore unless someone is cussing.

Engaging the World

Power Shift 2007 is just one example of how God is opening doors all around the world to his message of love and reconciliation. How can we move forward intentionally here?

Jesus calls his followers to be in the world but not of it. In other words, we are to remain distinct, but not isolated, from the rest of the world. On one hand, we must continue to stand firmly for Christ as the only savior for us and this planet. There will inevitably be pressure to downplay our exclusive claims to truth, and we must resist such demands. On the other hand, we have a lot to learn from the expertise and experience within the mainstream environmental movement.

I have a good friend who was involved as a leader in the Sierra Student Coalition for many years. He is the one who helped connect me to Power Shift and is also where I turn for helpful ideas and feedback on organizing new initiatives. Many others in organizations such as the Sierra Club and National Wildlife Federation have been accomplishing good work in caring for the planet for many years, while the church has been lagging behind. If all truth is God's truth, it is no surprise that he would choose to accomplish his will even through those who do not knowingly follow him yet—especially in an area where his church has been lagging behind.

The InterVarsity Christian Fellowship (IVCF) team at the University of Illinois–Urbana-Champaign campus understands this. In March 2008 they invited me to speak at their large-group meetings on the topic "Is God Green?" The University of Illinois is home to two sizable IVCF large groups—one for the Urbana campus and one for the Champaign campus—along with a ministry to the Greek community.

They were excited about hosting large-group talks on this theme because it provided both a challenge for them to grow in an important area of Christian discipleship and an opportunity to build bridges and engage with campus environmental groups that made no claim to faith. Based on the efforts of those IVCF leaders, here are five basic principles for how we can engage in creation care outside the church:

Pray constantly. Prayer—for peers in the environmental movement as well as for ourselves—is one of our most powerful but overlooked tools. The IVCF team leaders started praying for the talks far in advance. On the night of the talks, we gathered in the office before the session to pray together in person.

Understand one another. There are a lot of harmful and inaccurate stereotypes about both Christians and environmentalists. By intentionally trying to get to know each other, we can better understand the perspectives each of us is coming from and be sensitive to the limitations and weaknesses within the various communities. Student organizers from the IVCF chapters took the time to learn about and then visit the various environmental clubs meeting on their campus. While at the club meetings they also gave out personal invitations to the upcoming "Is God Green?" event.

Heal past hurts or frustrations. Damage has clearly been done to cause the church and the environmental community to view each other with so much distrust and derision. This resentment does not have to linger; we can recover a more honest, accurate and charitable view of each other. This can start with a humble and sincere apology for how Christians have been largely absent from environmental efforts (or even in opposition to them). While at the environmental club meetings, the IVCF student leaders were graciously given time to address the group. Commendably, the first thing out of their mouths was just such an apology.

Affirm and support the good work being done. The mainstream environmental movement needs our encouragement. When people and groups are doing God's work—even if they are not doing it for God or in his name—we can support their efforts. This is why the second thing that the IVCF student leaders did at the environmental club meetings was sincerely thank their classmates for what they were doing to care for the earth.

Find common ground. Regardless of how our views on issues like evolution differ, we all agree that the planet is in trouble and that we have lots of urgent work to do. This should be enough to get us going. The IVCF student leaders took the initiative here by offering to explore ways both groups could work together in the future.

These IVCF leaders put a lot of sincere thought and effort into reaching out beyond their group for the "Is God Green?" event. On the nights of the talks, though, it was unclear how many new faces actually showed up—not that many, according to their observations.

Still, relationships take time to develop. This is just the start of meaningful interactions between IVCF and the environmental groups on campus. I know it was not all in vain. On the first night I randomly sat next to a science student who had never been to an IVCF event before, but had come because she was interested in what Christians had to say about hugging trees.

Uplink: Ajith Fernando, National Director, Youth For Christ, Sri Lanka

Two Strands in the Bible

The primary aim in descriptions of the end times in the Bible is to help us live faithfully in the present. The Bible presents various strands of end-time events couched in figurative language that are sometimes difficult to harmonize, resulting in numerous debates about the end times. There are two such strands I want to discuss here. While we may not be able to harmonize them fully, both place before us some implications for action that we must take seriously.

The first is the strand that describes the earth being destroyed (see 2 Pet 3:10-13) and our final home being in "other-worldly" mansions (see Jn 14:1-6). Associated with this strand are those texts that teach that those who do not repent of their sin and those who are not born again will not enter the kingdom of God (see Jn 3:1-21; 1 Cor 6:9-11). These passages propel us to the work of evangelism that seeks to bring people to repentance, to receiving eternal salvation and to yielding to Christ's lordship. The Bible entertains

the hope of a great turning of large masses of people to Christ's salvation at the end of time (see Rom 11:25-32).

The second strand talks about the creation as being redeemed in the end. Texts describe the creation groaning, as in the pains of childbirth, as it awaits its redemption (see Rom 8:18-23); all creation being brought into a unity under Christ (see Eph 1:9-10; Col 1:20); and a day when all of the animal kingdom lives in harmony (see Is 11:6-8)—especially those humans living in perfect harmony under God (see Is 2:3-5). In case we think this is talking about a situation when the world will get better until all humanity is saved, our optimism is moderated by the fact that the context of both of the passages in Isaiah just cited is that of judgment.

I have been greatly encouraged by the statement "The glory and honor of the nations will be brought into [the new Jerusalem]" (see Rev 21:26). Something beautiful from Sri Lanka is going to be taken into the eternal kingdom. Sri Lanka is rapidly deteriorating, owing to corruption, violence and the ravages of an ethnic conflict. Life here is very frustrating and sometimes dangerous. Yet I am excited by the prospect of Sri Lanka contributing something glorious to the eternal kingdom. I am encouraged to stay on here and do my part in preparing that contribution. The prospect of a redeemed creation causes us to be committed to doing all we can to make this earth a better place.

Jesus said that God feeds the birds of the air and clothes the grass of the fields (see Mt 6:26-30). So when we care for the environment we are doing God's work. The original call for humans to care for the creation (see Gen 1:28) was not cancelled when we sinned, for it is repeated in the psalms (see Ps 8:6-8). However, in the passage just cited from Matthew, Jesus also said that humans are of greater value than plants and animals and that God is committed to feeding and clothing

them. This shows us the importance of meeting the material needs of humans (social concern). Elsewhere Jesus said that it doesn't profit a person to gain the whole world—that is, have all his or her material needs met—but to lose his own soul (see Mt 16:26). This shows how important evangelism is.

Does the argumentation above suggest that those doing social concern are more important than those committed to environmental concerns, or that those doing evangelism are more important than those doing social concern? The Bible does not teach such a hierarchy of service functions. But we can say that, while it is very important to be involved in protecting the environment and meeting human needs, we must guard against the natural tendency to neglect evangelism. Such a warning is especially relevant today because many in our pluralistic society frown upon evangelism.

Epilogue
A Revolution of Hope

Be joyful though you have considered all the facts.

Wendell Berry, "Manifesto: The Mad Farmer Liberation Front"

7:55 p.m., March 29, 2008: My three roommates and I stopped what we were doing. We powered down the computer, shut the heat off and turned the lights out. Grabbing some chairs and blankets, we bundled up in a circle on the grass outside our home. A friend happened to bring his visiting father by to meet us, so we ran back in for a couple more chairs and expanded the circle.

At 8:00 p.m., we turned our cell phones off. We were ready.

For the next sixty minutes, we joined millions of people all around the world in observing Earth Hour 2008 by stepping back from our energy-intensive lifestyles to save electricity and thus cut back on greenhouse gas emissions. Earth Hour is an annual event sponsored by the World Wildlife Fund on the last Saturday in March to highlight the challenges of global climate change.[1] The first Earth Hour was a Sydney affair in 2007, but in 2008 it quickly spread to Manila, Dublin, New York, San Francisco and beyond. As I write, Earth Hour 2009 is in the works.

Of course, given that the average American alone produces around 20 tons of carbon dioxide a year and that the entire world produces 27 billion tons of this greenhouse gas annually, turning the lights off for one hour is really not going to save enough carbon emissions to fix anything.[2] But Earth Hour is not being proposed as the solution; it is merely part of many ongoing efforts to build awareness and to demonstrate our collective commitment to pursue real solutions for climate change.

For the six of us that night, however, it was more than a symbolic gesture. It was also an opportunity to celebrate the abundance and beauty of life together, to slow down and take time to worship God in his creation. We brought a couple of guitars out and sang "This Is Our Father's World" and "All Creatures of Our God and King." We read from the Bible and from some of St. Francis's writings about creation.³ We prayed together in our little group.

And as we sat together, my mind wandered back to the conversation I'd had with Professor Mbutu in Kigoma, Tanzania, a couple of years earlier (as mentioned in the introduction). Walking with him back to our lodgings after dinner, we talked about the many problems facing the people of Kigoma. I had a strong feeling of hopelessness that night. Among other complexly interwoven issues, they were suffering from the effects of long-term environmental degradation and climate change. These huge problems stretch far beyond their ability to address alone, and certainly beyond mine. But still he challenged me: "When you go back to America, do not forget us," he said. "You must tell our story to your people."

So I did share their story. I told it in churches, youth groups, college campuses, conferences and in conversations all across the United States. I will continue to share their story whenever I can, because it pushes us to reimagine how we can better live together as God's people in his good but groaning creation.

Now, however, I also have a story of my own to share with Professor Mbutu.

It is our story.

It is the story of Goshen College (Indiana), which was recently awarded the highest possible LEED (Leadership in Energy and Environmental Design) rating—platinum—for its Merry Lea Environmental Learning Center. About seven thousand students, ranging from preschoolers to college graduates, pass through Merry Lea's diverse educational and research programs annually.⁴ This recognition officially makes Merry Lea the first platinum-rated building in Indiana and certifies that it was constructed and operates as sustainably as possible.

It is the story of A Rocha UK, which partnered with local groups in the largely immigrant Southhall neighborhood of London to rehabilitate a ninety-acre wasteland full of junked cars and pollution. This previously trashed land has now been transformed into the Minet Country Park, with natural areas that welcome wildlife (including more than one hundred species of birds) and recreational spaces for the community to host cultural and educational events.

It is the story of Messiah College, Wheaton Chinese Alliance Church, the Renewal network, Fuller Theological Seminary, Vineyard Boise, The Simple Way and countless other communities all over the United States, and in fact throughout the world, who are urgently coming together to shine the light of Christ into the dark crises of creation. It is a developing story that I have tried to convey in these pages—of lives changed, land healed and relationships renewed. On our own, many of these challenges were beyond our reach; together, we are increasingly able to meet them head-on. As Professor Mbutu's story challenges us, so I hope our story will encourage him.

Real Hope

Of course, what if this is all just wishful thinking or "hope mongering"? Even if we are joining together to tackle the crises of today, are we ultimately going to be able to fix things in time? The world is in such a mess. Do we still stand a real chance?

I hear these questions a lot, and I can certainly relate to the feeling. It's easy to feel overwhelmed by all the evil and trouble around and within us. Our response to this bleak state of affairs, however, is one of the most visible distinctions between those who are of Christ and those who are of the world.

The world sees the state of the planet today and is filled with despair and driven to action out of fear and desperation. Followers of Christ, with our eyes fixed on Jesus, see the same issues, but are filled with hope and driven by his love—his love for us and for all that he has created and cherishes.

I believe that the bleakest moment in all of time has already occurred. It was the moment when the Son of God suffered and died on a cross.

Everything we have been through since he resurrected in victory and anything we may yet face in the future can still be indescribably dark. But it will never again be as dark as it was when Christ took his last breath. Things are, in truth, actually looking up.

This does not mean all is well and we can ease off. Instead, it means we can press onward together with great hope and joy. For, as Christ was not bound by the tomb, so we need not be bound by despair.[5] In the hope of his resurrection, we know that the work we do is part of God's cause and that he will take all our imperfect efforts toward completion in Christ's return. Richard Foster sums up our situation well:

> We over-eat, over-buy, and over-build, spewing out our toxic wastes upon the earth and into the air. But this gloomy picture is not the final word. Hope has the final word. We are not locked into a prison of determinism: change is possible. Ruthless inequities can be eradicated. The hungry can be fed. Millions can be reached with the message of life in Christ. He whose power is over all desires to use his people as agents of change. We are to walk cheerfully over the face of the earth, conquering evil with good in the power of the Spirit.[6]

Our calling is to remain faithful to him; his promise is to bring his reign of shalom on earth.

God's Dream

In the United States, and increasingly throughout the world, the prevailing vision that everyone strives for is the American Dream. It is the promise that anyone who works hard enough can expect to find success, comfort and happiness in life. This offers hope to a society and world that is, by and large, still very needy and searching for something better.

It is, however, an empty promise with false expectations. The fabled American Dream fuels the narcissistic pursuit of wealth and convenience that has led to our current addiction to consumption; it is not a dream worth pursuing. Many will work hard all their lives chasing this goal and never be rewarded. The few who do find wealth and status will never be truly happy or at peace.

There is another, better dream to strive for. It is the vision that John the apostle was given of the kingdom of God when it comes in all fullness. Unlike the American Dream, this one is trustworthy and brings wholeness and healing:

> Then the angel showed me the river of the water of life, as clear as crystal, flowing from the throne of God and of the Lamb down the middle of the great street of the city. On each side of the river stood the tree of life, bearing twelve crops of fruit, yielding its fruit every month. And the leaves of the tree are for the healing of the nations. No longer will there be any curse. The throne of God and of the Lamb will be in the city, and his servants will serve him. They will see his face, and his name will be on their foreheads. There will be no more night. They will not need the light of a lamp or the light of the sun, for the Lord God will give them light. And they will reign for ever and ever. (Rev 22:1-5)

Amen. There can be no greater hope than this.

And so we press on joyfully because God has given us a vision of eternity that drowns out any pessimism in the present. We are able to boldly tackle environmental crises without being overwhelmed, because we know that our success lies in God, and that it is secure.

So let us serve together purposefully and with great joy. Let us excel at proclaiming and showing God's love to one another and to all that he has placed in our care. And let us always be ready to give an account for the hope we profess (see Heb 10:23; 1 Pet 3:15).

The grace and peace of Jesus Christ be with you, and all praise be to God.

Afterword
J. Matthew Sleeth, M.D.

Last fall Ben Lowe and I were traveling together. We arrived at a Christian liberal arts college where I was to give the morning chapel and Ben the evening one. Ben had parked his compact, hybrid car in a remote corner of the parking lot—under a tree and beside a hedge. He donned a tie and jacket. I brushed my teeth and spit in the bushes.

Ben looked from himself, to me, and back. He broke into his characteristic, good-natured laugh and declared, "We're *so* missionary." This was high praise coming from a pastor's son who has contracted malaria, tuberculosis and giardia while serving in remote corners of the globe.

I suppose that, in some measure, anyone who ventures from home to bring the good news to those who have not heard it is, by definition, a missionary. But what is the "good news"? Many have seen people waving "John 3:16 banners" from the bleachers at football stadiums and even at wrestling matches. The verse—that God loves the world so much that he was willing to give his most precious thing, his son, to save it—stirs the hearts of believers. But the next verse—that God sent his son into the world, not to destroy it but to save and redeem it—is equally compelling. Together they are the Good News with a Plan.

I think it is fair to say that both believers in God and nonbelievers feel that something is not quite right in the world. The believer has the third chapter of Genesis (the Fall) to support this view. The nonbeliever might point to war, greed and pollution to make his case. The question is "What will we do about it?"

Ben proposes a green revolution, and I agree. Christianity is not a simple faith. It is complicated. On more than one occasion, crowds turned from Jesus in confusion and disgust. I recently told my son, who is studying medicine, "Real things aren't simple." A revolution that synthesizes environmental concerns and the principles of life that Jesus taught will not be simple either, but it is what the Bible tells us to do. The Good News with a Plan uses people of faith as the arms, legs, minds and wills of its operation.

Years ago, when I began traveling to teach about the Bible and the connection to creation care, it was tough going. But things are changing. I can no longer hope to meet all the requests to preach, teach and write about the green revolution. A new generation, Ben's, has taken up this vital mission. Millions more must join.

Today, few question that there are looming environmental problems. A look at the air above most metropolitan areas in the world confirms that the sky is polluted. Signs warning of dioxin and mercury in fish remind us of the legacy of water contamination. Some countries have it worse, and a few have it better, but the size of our world is rapidly shrinking. There is no "away." We, and our children, will eventually eat, drink or breathe everything we throw "away." The concept of sin haunting families for generations is not new. It is as old as Genesis, as specific as the Ten Commandments, and as real as cancer and asthma.

Certainly the word *revolution* conjures some bad events in history. The French, Russian and Chinese revolutions are examples of times when innocent blood was wantonly shed. However, other revolutions are more benign—or at least less bloody. We as individuals, churches and nations have the bad habit of looking at others and judging. Christ cracked a carpentry joke about this habit: "Do not judge, or you too will be judged," he said. "Get the two-by-four out of your own eye before you worry about the dust mote in your neighbor's eye" (Mt 7:1-4, my paraphrase).

It is all too tempting to look at others and see their sins clearly, while remaining blind to our own. The revolution to which Christ invites his followers begins with a personal transformation. Having read Ben's book, think about what you can do to change, to become a better steward of God's world. Your neighbor may have a gigantic SUV and leave mountains of aluminum cans to be carried off on trash day, but what about that flight to Europe you took last year to go hiking?

Ultimately, revolutions are either won or lost. It remains to be seen what the outcome of the green revolution will be. The enemy is not a corporation or country. The enemy is greed, thoughtlessness and wishful (magical) thinking. The enemy will confront you when you wash your face in the morning. But, by God's grace, the hero of this revolution can also be found in the mirror.

In his letter to the Romans, Paul described the church as being a body with many parts. He advised that each of us use the gifts we are given to make the world a place where God's will is done. For that reason, he also advised that we not "conform" ourselves to the worldly goals of gain and fame.

May all who read this book find inspiration to do their part in bringing the kingdom of heaven to earth today. May you become *"so missionary"* that God will declare you a "good and faithful servant" (Mt 25:21, 23).

Appendix A
Good Books

The resources in these appendixes—books, websites and organizations—are ones I've found especially meaningful. In some cases, I may not entirely agree with some of their positions or projects, but have found enough value in them to recommend them to others.

Berry, R. J., ed. *The Care of Creation: Focusing Concern and Action.* Leicester, U.K.: Inter-Varsity Press, 2000.

Bobo, Kim, Jackie Kendall and Steve Max. *Organizing for Social Change: Midwest Academy Manual for Activists.* 3rd ed. Santa Ana, Calif.: Seven Locks Press, 2001.

Bookless, Dave. *Planetwise: Dare to Care for God's World.* Nottingham, U.K.: Inter-Varsity Press, 2008.

Bouma-Prediger, Steven. *For the Beauty of the Earth: A Christian View for Creation Care.* Grand Rapids: Baker Academic, 2001.

Brandt, Don, ed. *God's Stewards: The Role of Christians in Creation Care.* Monrovia, Calif.: World Vision International, 2002.

Brower, Michael, and Warren Leon. *The Consumer's Guide to Effective Environmental Choices: Practical Advice from the Union of Concerned Scientists.* New York: Three Rivers Press, 1999.

Brown, Edward R. *Our Father's World: Mobilizing the Church to Care for Creation.* Downers Grove, Ill.: InterVarsity Press, 2008.

Brown, Michael Jacoby. *Building Powerful Community Organizations: A Personal Guide to Creating Groups That Can Solve Problems and Change the World.* Arlington, Mass.: Long Haul Press, 2006.

Davis, Brangien, and Katharine Wroth, ed. *Wake Up and Smell the Planet: The Non-Pompous, Non-Preachy Grist Guide to Greening Your Day.* Seattle: Mountaineers Books, 2007.

DeWitt, Calvin. *Earth-Wise: A Biblical Response to Environmental Issues.* 2nd ed. Grand Rapids: Faith Alive Christian Resources, 2007.

Harris, Peter. *Kingfisher's Fire: A Story of Hope for God's Earth*. Oxford: Monarch Books, 2008.

Harris, Peter. *Under the Bright Wings*. Vancouver, B.C.: Regent College Publishing, 2000

Hodson, Martin J., and Margot R. Hodson. *Cherishing the Earth: How to Care for God's Creation*. Oxford: Monarch Books, 2008.

Houghton, Sir John. *Global Warming: The Complete Briefing*. Cambridge, Mass.: Cambridge University Press, 1997.

Isham, Jonathan, and Sissel Waage, ed. *Ignition: What You Can Do to Fight Global Warming and Spark a Movement*. Washington, D.C.: Island Press, 2007.

McKibben, Bill. *Deep Economy: The Wealth of Communities and the Durable Future*. New York: Times Books, 2007.

Monbiot, George. *Heat: How to Stop the Planet from Burning*. Cambridge, Mass.: South End Press, 2007.

Robinson, Tri, and Jason Chatraw. *Saving God's Green Earth: Rediscovering the Church's Responsibility to Environmental Stewardship*. Norcross, Ga.: Ampelon Publishing, 2006.

Schaeffer, Francis A. *Pollution and the Death of Man: The Christian View of Ecology*. Wheaton, Ill.: Tyndale, 1970.

Scott, Lindy, ed. *Christians, the Care of Creation, and Global Climate Change*. Eugene, Ore.: Pickwick Publications, 2008.

Sleeth, Emma. *It's Easy Being Green: One Student's Guide to Serving God and Saving the Planet*. Grand Rapids: Zondervan, 2008.

Sleeth, Matthew. *Serve God, Save the Planet: A Christian Call to Action*. Grand Rapids: Zondervan, 2007.

Tillett, Sarah, ed. *Caring for Creation: Biblical and Theological Perspectives*. Abingdon, U.K.: Bible Reading Fellowship, 2005.

Valerio, Ruth. *L Is for Lifestyle: Christian Living that Doesn't Cost the Earth*. Leicester, England: Inter-Varsity Press, 2004.

Van Dyke, Fred, David C. Mahan, Joseph K. Sheldon and Raymond H. Brand. *Redeeming Creation: The Biblical Basis for Environmental Stewardship*. Downers Grove, Ill.: InterVarsity Press, 1996.

Appendix B
Helpful Websites

Deep Green Conversation: An interactive site with content, resources and a blog that integrates the Christian faith with a "deep green lifestyle." <www.deepgreenconversation.org>

American Scientific Affiliation (ASA): Founded in 1941, the ASA is a fellowship of Christians in science-related disciplines. Its website has many helpful resources and papers on topics ranging from environmentalism to theories of origins. <www.asa3.org>

Evangelical Climate Initiative (ECI): The ECI website contains helpful resources on climate change from a Christian perspective, along with an updated list of signatories. It explains what this groundbreaking initiative is about and provides resources for getting involved. <www.christiansandclimate.org>

Re:Vision, National Association of Evangelicals: A useful tool of their Re:Vision campaign, this website contains resources for understanding and taking action on creation care, as well as links to other good sites. <www.revision.org>

National Council of Churches (NCC) Eco-Justice Programs: Many good programs, resources and opportunities available through the NCC and its member denominations. Many denominations (both evangelical and mainline Protestant) have their own statements, programs and resources as well. <www.nccecojustice.org>

Grist: A hugely popular independent environmental news and commentary site based out of Seattle, but with strong national appeal. Well worth checking out.
<www.grist.org>

Treehugger: Another leading media outlet focused on empowering environmental sustainability through news, blogs, articles, product reviews and much more.
<www.treehugger.com>

BBC News "Science/Nature": The place to find the latest news on all things related to the planet, ranging from new species discoveries to environmental policy breakthroughs and much more. Also contains helpful overviews for key issues, such as climate change.
<http://news.bbc.co.uk/2/hi/science/nature/default.stm>

RealClimate: Do you have questions about the latest juicy climate-change controversy you heard on the news or from friends? Here is "a commentary site on climate science by working climate scientists for the interested public and journalists." Engaging, accessible and avowedly nonpolitical.
<www.realclimate.org>

Riverwired: An online community and central clearinghouse for all things related to green living. Organized into many helpful categories and includes original videos, blogs, networking opportunities and lots of other useful features.
<www.riverwired.com>

Gogreentube: An unrelated spin-off of YouTube for videos specifically related to the environment.
<www.gogreentube.com>

Creation, I Care: A website put together by a task force at Northland, A Church Distributed in Longwood, Florida. It includes many helpful resources geared toward evangelical churches, including teachings by their senior pastor, Dr. Joel Hunter, testimonies from church members

about caring for creation, and a report of the internal environmental audit on their church campus.
<www.creationicare.net>

Let's Tend the Garden: Another good example of what a church ministry dedicated to creation care can do. Let's Tend the Garden is part of the Vineyard Boise church, led by Pastor Tri Robinson. This website contains thoughtful essays, a short but compelling film of the ministry, information about ways they are engaging in creation care, recordings of past environmental stewardship conferences and listings of future events.
<www.letstendthegarden.org>

Santa Barbara A Rocha: A community chapter of A Rocha that can be found online.
<www.arochasb.org>

Select websites for campus creation care groups:

Northwestern College (Iowa): *Terra Nova Ecology Club*
<http://home.nwciowa.edu/terra/home.htm>

Judson College (Alabama): *Cahaba River Society Chapter*
<www.wilsonbiology.info/cahabariver.htm>

Calvin College (Michigan): *Environmental Stewardship Coalition*
<http://clubs.calvin.edu/esc>

Goshen College (Indiana): *Merry Lea Environmental Learning Center*
<www.goshen.edu/merrylea>; *EcoPax* student group <www.goshen.edu/clubs/ecopax>; *Topics on the Environment* student group <www.goshen.edu/clubs/tote>

College groups affiliated with A Rocha USA: Asbury, Grace College, Grove City, Ohio State, Westmont, Wheaton (websites available through the U.S. pages at <www.arocha.org>)

Appendix C
Organizations Involved in Creation Care

A Rocha—Christians in Conservation: See appendix D.

Au Sable Institute of Environmental Studies: The Au Sable Institute has four campuses that offer training and courses in environmental fields from a distinctly Christian perspective. The institute has been a cornerstone in the creation care movement because it has served as the training ground and central networking site for Christian students and faculty from all around the country. Many colleges and universities in the Council of Christian Colleges and Universities also apply credits earned at one of the Au Sable Institute campuses directly toward their students' major requirements. <www.ausable.org>

Care of Creation: Led by Ed Brown, author of *Our Father's World*, Care of Creation is a Christian environmental missions organization. Their focus is to mobilize the church to address environmental issues facing their communities and their neighbors around the world. They do this through writing, speaking and consultations. In Kenya, Care of Creation has an active project located in Limuru that focuses on farming, tree planting and water harvesting. <www.careofcreation.org>

Creation Care Study Program (CCSP): CCSP offers semester-long study-abroad programs taught by Christian professors in Belize and New Zealand/Samoa. Academic credit obtained through CCSP is usually easily transferable at Christian colleges, which makes it an attractive option for students who want to spend a focused semester immersed in creation care outside their home institutions. <www.creationcsp.org>

Christians for the Mountains: Christians for the Mountains is a grassroots organization working to end the practice of mountaintop removal mining (MTR) in Appalachia. Led by Allen Johnson, they work to engage churches and raise awareness nationally on many of the issues surrounding MTR. Christians for the Mountains partners closely with other organizations, such as the Ohio Valley Environmental Coalition and Coal River Mountain Watch and has put together a series of short documentary films on a DVD titled *Mountain Mourning*. <www.christiansforthemountains.org>

Earth Ministry: This ministry in the Pacific Northwest works with churches to engage communities on environmental concerns. They also put together helpful resources for use in churches and maintain a website that lists lots of information and events. <www.earthministry.org>

Ecological Concerns for Hunger Organization (ECHO): A leader in sustainable agricultural practices, ECHO is a Christian missions and consulting organization based out of North Ft. Myers, Flordia. A member of the Association of Evangelical Relief and Development Organizations, ECHO's mission is "to network with community leaders in developing countries to seek hunger solutions for families growing food under difficult conditions." Their Florida headquarters includes a nursery, seed bank and global demonstration farm, which also doubles as the Florida campus of the Au Sable Institute. Interested students and graduates can also intern in different areas of the organization, where they learn hands-on sustainable agriculture practices for a wide variety of ecosystems. <www.echonet.org>

Evangelical Environmental Network (EEN): The EEN is based out of Washington, D.C., and Atlanta, and seeks to "educate, inspire, and mobilize Christians in their effort to care for God's creation, to be faithful stewards of God's provision, and to advocate for actions and policies that honor God and protect the environment." Their website contains many biblically based resources geared toward a range of ages and audiences, and they publish *Creation Care* quarterly. <www.creationcare.org>

Floresta: Their mission is to "reverse deforestation and poverty in the world, by transforming the lives of the rural poor." They do this through community development education, agriculture and forestry, microfinance loans, and Christian discipleship. They currently have projects on the ground in Tanzania, Haiti, Mexico and the Dominican Republic, along with offices in the United States. <www.floresta.org>

Renewal—Students Caring for Creation: See appendix E.

Restoring Eden: Peter Illyn leads this advocacy outreach organization based in Washington state. He frequently speaks on campuses and at conferences, raising awareness and enthusiasm for creation care. Restoring Eden is also a member of the Energy Action Coalition, a diverse gathering of environmental organizations dedicated to addressing the climate crisis. <www.restoringeden.org>

Appendix D

A ROCHA

Christians in Conservation

A Rocha is an international conservation organization caring for God's world—and we'd love to work with you.

The news is bad and getting worse. Species extinct. Habitats destroyed. Disease. Poverty. Famine. Creation groans.

But there is hope.

The God who created the world, called it very good and sacrificed his Son to redeem it is still at work. And so are we.

Since our beginning in 1983 in Portugal—where A Rocha [ah RAW sha] means "the rock"—we've been conducting scientific research, doing hands-on fieldwork, running education programs and inviting Christians and all others to join us in heeding the Bible's call to lovingly steward the earth. Now at work in eighteen countries on six continents, A Rocha is a worldwide family of community-led conservation efforts.

We invite you to join us. A Rocha community groups, field study centers, student efforts and volunteer opportunities are a great way to get involved and share the load—and the blessing.

A Rocha USA contact information:
e-mail: usa@arocha.org
call: 830 990-7940
write: P.O. Box 1338, Fredericksburg, TX 78624, USA
go to: <www.arocha.org>

A Rocha USA, Inc., is a tax-exempt 501(c)(3) organization registered in the United States, and is part of the worldwide A Rocha family.

Appendix E

"To inspire and equip the student generation to lead its communities with justice and compassion in Christ-centered stewardship of all of God's creation."

Renewal is a grassroots network of Christian students and recent graduates that focuses on living in right relationship with God.

Across the United States and Canada, we are joining together to follow Christ's example of love, stewardship and reconciliation. For us, this means taking care of everything that God so lovingly created—the earth and each other.

With a heart for the poor and a commitment to Jesus' call to love your neighbor as yourself, the students of Renewal seek to actively care for the earth so that all God's creatures, as well as future generations, can have a healthy environment to thrive in.

Check us out online at <www.renewingcreation.org> to find out more about who we are, what we're up to and how you can join the movement.

Acknowledgments

A book about the vitality of Christian community and its significance for how we live on this planet—which is what this aspires to be—really has to come out of Christian community. So, there are many unseen coauthors—family, friends, colleagues and mentors whose names do not appear on the cover but whose wisdom and stories are manifested throughout the pages. Without their valuable contributions to my life and manuscript, this book would have been no more engaging than the installation guide for a ceiling fan. And probably less practical too.

So, my love and deep gratitude to all—from Singapore and Malaysia to Tanzania and North America—who can be incriminated for helping me in one way or another. May God give you favor for being a blessing to me and for your many contributions toward the care of his creation.

A special shout out to . . .

Mom, Dad, Nat and Gram, for being family, guarding my writing space and encouraging me through the process. If there were a second dedication for this book, it would have to go to you.

My roommates and accountability partners during this intense experience: Ryan Cherry, Jonathan Kindberg and Jeremy Williams. With memories of the turtles upstairs, ramen-fests, yellow mellow, bed bugs, Chinese buffets, leaky air mattresses, driving overnight through blizzards and many other adventures. My heart is full of love for you poop-heads.

The Heinze family—for the opportunity to finish my time at Wheaton, without which none of this would have happened.

The Norregaard family—for being a terrific adopted family at WCAC and for all the good food, overflowing hospitality and spacious storage.

Fred (and Linda) Van Dyke, for taking me under your wing as adviser, mentor and, now, valued colleague.

Bruce, Catherine and Annika Norquist, for all the ice cream, enviro-talk, mentoring and friendship through this time.

Vince and Ellen Morris—for always speaking too highly of me, putting me up, baking desserts, giving sound advice and so much more.

The Cherrys, Wathens, Kindbergs, McCulloughs, Diane Garvin and Marilyn Brenner—for welcoming me as family and making special efforts to care.

Chris Gregory, Katie Fast, James Fischer, Jennifer Carver, Kelly Fisher, Henry Kuo, Hannah Mudge, Michelle and Dar Heinze, Val Paurus, Rae Wathen, Christy Page, Braden Koenigsberg, Karen Kihlstrom, Kenlee Valleskey, Amy Dykstra, James Cho, Jonathan May, Devin Ryan, Paul Lowe, Art Pogensky, Michael King, Nathan Wahl, Gabe Clemmons, Matt Soerens, Sean Sales, Malcolm Smillie, and Kami Keith—for encouragement in the writing process and providing personal support when it mattered a lot. You remembered, cared, celebrated and were patient when I was often scatterbrained and under pressure to meet deadlines.

The highly talented Wheaton Summit Task Force: Lisa Riihimaki (who also provided helpful feedback on the final draft of this book), Jennifer Luedtke, Lisa Jutsum, Brittney Dunn, Hannah Walters, Glenn Sharman, Reed Fagan and Brendan Payne. What a team!

My family at A Rocha—the A Rocha USA Board, Tom Rowley, Dan Harper, Ginny Vroblesky, the Sprengers, Markku Kostamo, Rick Faw, Peter Harris, Marie Connett-Porceddu, Melissa Ong and Daniel Tay, Barbara Mearns, Rosie Rutherford, Dave Bookless, Will Simonson, Julió Reïs, Simon and Ann Stuart, Elizabeth Whitworth, Rich Dixon, Marty Robertson, John Humphreys, Don Bosch, Matt Wistrand, Shelly Thomas, Carol Kuniholm, Micah Bennett, and others.

My family at Wheaton—Jeff Greenberg (thanks especially for giving me time to write the proposal), Kristen Page, Nadine Folino Rorem, Jim Clark, Steve "Doc Mo" Moshier, Noah Toly, P. J. Hill, Lindy Scott, Vince Bacote, David Cook, Steve Kellough, Duane Litfin, Dorothy Chappell, Vicki Totel, Steve Ivester, Doug DeMerchant, Lori Hart, Sarah Clark, Sam Shellhammer, Rich Powers, Paul Chelsen, Betsey Green, members of the Environmental Stewardship Advisory Committee, A Rocha Wheaton and Earthkeepers, Reslife Upperclass Hall Staff 05-06 and 06-07, and the guys of Evans 2.

Wheaton Chinese Alliance Church, pastors Michael Green and Ben Tzeng—for being my home church, nurturing me in faith, giving me a place to serve and supporting me in ministry. Youth group rocks!

Darryl Chew, fellow school captain—for duty rosters, room rugby and faithful friendship over many years.

Matthew, Nancy, Emma and Clark Sleeth—for valuable help and encouragement with the book.

Shane Claiborne—for your enthusiastic support and for writing the foreword.

Many thanks to those who contributed uplinks and dispatches, and have not yet been mentioned, including Will Samson, Paul Corts, Bettie Ann Brigham, Janel Curry, Ed Johnson, Dorothy Boorse, Jonathan Merritt, Ajith Fernando, Allen Johnson, Dustin Ford and Thad Salmon. You cheerfully took the time to support a young tyke, and I am very grateful.

My patient project editor, Al Hsu, along with Andy Le Peau, Jeff and Cindy Crosby, Ruth Curphey, Peter Mayer, and other helpful staff at InterVarsity Press who trusted me with a contract and then took my ramblings and expertly fashioned them into a book.

Beau Friedlander—for helping me navigate through the unknown contract process.

Anonymous reviewers and copyeditors—only you know just how much work the book needed after the early drafts. Thanks for the many helpful comments and pardon any remaining weaknesses.

Thanks also to the friends and colleagues whose warm hospitality, expert counsel and inspiring testimonies have given me many stories and ideas to share in this book:

Andy and Katie Bathje, Art and Evie McPhee, and Megan and Chris Estelle, at Asbury College and Asbury Seminary; Doug Allen and Teresa Maas at Dordt College; Laurel Kearns at Drew University; Dave Hoferer, Dave Unander, Stan LeQuire, Emily Brown, Tyler Sheaffer and the Earthkeepers at Eastern University; Mat Schetne and Madeline Skillen at Gordon College; Paul Steury at Goshen College; Curtis Valasek, Drew Rochotte, Eileen Boekestein and the enthusiastic members of Fostering Eden/A Rocha Grace at Grace College and Seminary; Lori Gaffner and the welcoming folks at Greenville College; Melissa and Brian Danielson, John and Tera Dent, Stanley Keehlwetter, Donna Cales and members of the E-Club/A Rocha Grove City, for one of my most memorable campus visits; Kim Phipps, Erik Lindquist, Dave Foster, Lauren Kras, Amanda McMillan, members of Earthkeepers, and Restoration House at Messiah College; Jonathan Bosma at Michigan Tech University; Greg Hitzhusen and Ben Thrasher at Ohio State University—for breaking new ground with A Rocha OSU; David Clark, Mike Steger, Kevin Abel, Thomas Chesnes and Gary Parker at Palm Beach Atlantic; Susan Drake Emmerich at Trinity Christian College; Karen Steensma, David Clements, Melissa Oakes and Trish Buhler at Trinity Western University; Rachel Keung and the InterVarsity staff at University of Illinois Urbana-Champaign; Ann Lowe, Julia Johnson and members of A Rocha Westmont at Westmont College; Kevin "Flavio" Sloat and the good folks at Epic-Remix; Joel Hunter, Raymond Randall and Bob Giguere at Northland, A Church Distributed; Paul Corts, Jennifer Byrnes, Rich Gathro, Ron Mahurin, Nate Mouttet and Ryan Moede at the CCCU; Richard Cizik at the National Association of Evangelicals; Matthew Anderson-Stembridge at the Creation Care Fund; Dean Ohlman from RBC; Ed Brown at Care of Creation; Allen Johnson and Sage Russo at Christians for the Mountains; John Wood and Dave Mahan at the Au Sable Institute; Jim Ball, Rusty Pritchard, Jim Jewell, Alexei Laushkin and Kendra Juskus at the EEN; Ben Campbell at Conservation International; Ryan Hobert at the U.N. Foundation; Bill McKibben at Middlebury College; Melanie Griffin, Lyndsay Moseley, Anna Jane Joyner, Nathan Wyeth and Jared Duvall at the Sierra Club; Kara Ball, Lisa Madry and Justin Schott at the National Wildlife Federation; and Friends at Vineyard Boise and Let's Tend the Garden.

Notes

Introduction: Why a Revolution?

[1]This and other statistics on the global water situation are available from Water Partners International <http://water.org/waterpartners.aspx?pgID=916>.

[2]The whale story was largely inspired by "The Star Thrower," an essay by Loren Eiseley (1907-1977).

[3]This assertion was made in two extensive geological surveys reported in 2004 and 2008. News releases of these studies can be read at <www.sciencedaily.com/releases/2008/01/080125100314.htm> and <www.sciencedaily.com/releases/2004/11/041103234736.htm>.

[4]Richard J. Foster, *Freedom of Simplicity* (New York: HarperCollins, 1981), p. 146.

Chapter 1: Incompatible Foolishness

[1]This statistic and the previous four were obtained from "GEO-4," the fourth report in the Global Environment Outlook series, published by the United Nations Environment Program (UNEP) in 2008. "GEO-4" was prepared by about 390 experts around the world, reviewed by more than a thousand others, and is available online at <www.unep.org/geo/>.

[2]Data on biodiversity come from the World Wildlife Fund's Living Planet Report available online at <www.panda.org/livingplanet/>, and the International Union for Conservation of Nature and Natural Resources's Red List of Threatened Species available online at <www.iucnredlist.org/>.

[3]Data on deforestation come from "The State of the World's Forests 2007," published by the Food and Agriculture Organization of the United Nations in 2007 and available online at <www.fao.org/docrep/009/a0773e/a0773e00.htm>.

[4]More specific projections on the impacts of global climate change can be found through the 2007 Nobel Peace Prize–winning Intergovernmental Panel on Climate Change website <www.ipcc.ch/>.

[5]Data on poverty come from the "Human Development Report 2007/2008" published by the United Nations Development Program, available at <http://hdr.undp.org/en/reports/global/hdr2007-2008/>.

[6]This assertion was made in an essay by Michael Shellenberger and Ted Nordhaus titled "The Death of Environmentalism." First released at the October 2004 meeting of the Environmental Grantmakers Association, the full report can be downloaded at <www.thebreakthrough.org/images/Death_ of_Environmentalism.pdf>.

[7]Attributed to Gus Speth, dean of the Yale School of Forestry and Environmental Studies. It was shared by Rev. Richard Cizik, vice president of governmental affairs of the National Association of Evangelicals, during his plenary speech to the 2007 Environmental Stewardship Conference at Vineyard Boise church. A transcript of the talk can be found at <http://www.letstendthegarden.org/conference/2007conference.htm>.

[8]The reference to society as a "suicidal system" is attributed to fellow author Leonard Sweet by Brian McLaren in *Everything Must Change: Jesus, Global Crises, and a Revolution of Hope* (Nashville: Nelson, 2007).

[9]Mark Gornik, *To Live in Peace: Biblical Faith and the Changing Inner City* (Grand Rapids: Eerdmans, 2002), p. 101.

[10]Personal communication received on April 15, 2007; source kept anonymous to avoid compromising their ability to minister effectively in their community.

[11]Francis Schaeffer and Udo Middelmann, *Pollution and the Death of Man* (Wheaton, Ill.: Crossway Books, 1992).

[12]Cornelius Plantinga Jr., *Not the Way It's Supposed to Be: A Breviary of Sin* (Grand Rapids: Eerdmans, 1995), pp. 14-16.

[13]Ban Ki-Moon, "The Right War," *Time*, April 16, 2008 <www.time.com/time/specials/2007/environment/article/0,28804,1730759_1731383_1731345,00.html>.

[14]Ibid.

[15]Rev. Peter Harris (creation care speech, Wheaton College Chapel, Wheaton, Ill., March 29, 2008).

Chapter 2: Prodigal Treehuggers

[1]This practical suggestion came from Edward R. Brown, *Our Father's World: Mobilizing the Church to Care for Creation* (Downers Grove, Ill.: InterVarsity Press, 2008), p. 139.

[2]Personal communication received in October 2007.

[3]My understanding of the implications of being created in God's image to creation care has been largely influenced by Vincent E. Morris, "Eighth-Day Creators: A Christian Environmental Stewardship Ethic Based on the 'Image of God' in the Doctrine of Creation" (Ph.D. dissertation, Department of Biblical and Theological Studies, Wheaton College Graduate School, Wheaton, Ill., 2006).

[4]Nicholas Wolterstorff, *Until Justice and Peace Embrace* (Grand Rapids: Eerdmans, 1983), p. 72.

[5]More information on the ACUPCC, including the statement, updated signatory list and news bulletins, can be found at <www.presidentsclimatecommitment.org/>.

[6]For more information on Audubon's annual Christmas Bird Count, including information on how to participate in your area, go to <www.audubon.org/bird/cbc/>.

Chapter 3: From Insulation to Incarnation

[1] Author and poet Wendell Berry has developed the theme of the connection between humans, community and the land throughout many of his writings.

[2] Energy Information Administration <www.eia.doe.gov/neic/quickfacts/quickcoal.html>.

[3] From the Environmental Protection Agency <www.epa.gov/waterscience/fish/advisories/2006/index.html>.

[4] From the Clean Air Task Force <www.catf.us/publications/reports/Children_at_Risk.pdf>.

[5] "Dirty Air, Dirty Power: Mortality and Health Damage Due to Air Pollution from Power Plants," Clean Air Task Force (June 2004) <www.catf.us/publications/view/24>.

[6] From Mountain Justice Summer <http://mountainjustice.org/facts/property.php>.

[7] From William Wilberforce's first speech in the British Parliament describing the slave trade, 1789, quoted by Rep. Frank Wolf of Virginia speaking to the U.S. House of Representatives, "We Cannot Say We Did Not Know," 5th sess., *Congressional Record* (April 10, 2008) <www.govtrack.us/congress/record.xpd?id=110-h20080410-55>.

Chapter 4: The Heat Is On

[1] The BBC has summarized this and other climate change statistics at <http://news.bbc.co.uk/2/hi/science/nature/portal/climate_change/default.stm>.

[2] Shaoni Bhattacharya, "European heatwave causes 35, 000 deaths," *New Scientist,* October 10, 2003 <www.newscientist.com/article/dn4259-european-heatwave-caused-35000-deaths.html>.

[3] From the Intergovernmental Panel on Climate Change <www.ipcc.ch/>.

[4] This and other information on the impacts of climate change in the United States is available through the "Scientific Assessment of the Effects of Global Change on the United States," released in May 2008 by the Office of Science and Technology Policy, Executive Office of the President. For the full report, see <http://www.ostp.gov/galleries/NSTC%20Reports/Scientific%20Assessment%20FULL%20Report.pdf>.

[5] A more in-depth look into the science of climate can be found in Sir John Houghton, *Global Warming: The Complete Briefing,* 3rd ed. (Cambridge: Cambridge University Press, 2004).

[6] The references here and throughout this chapter are taken from the 2007 IPCC Synthesis report unless otherwise noted (see note three in this chapter).

[7] From personal communication with geology professor Jim Clark at Wheaton College.

[8]This was before *An Inconvenient Truth,* the global-warming documentary featuring Al Gore, was released in 2006. Now most of the questions I get about global warming have something to do with the former vice president.

[9]C. M. O'Reilly, et al., "Climate change decreases aquatic ecosystem productivity of Lake Tanganyika," *Nature* 424 (2003): 766-68.

[10]The full statement and signatory list can be found at <www.creationcare.org/resources/declaration.php>.

[11]The What Would Jesus Drive? campaign can be found at <www.whatwould jesusdrive.org/>.

[12]More on the Oxford declaration, along with the statement, can be found at <www.jri.org.uk/news/statement.htm>.

[13]The Sandy Cove Covenant can be found at <www.creationcare.org/conference/>.

[14]The NAE's Re:Vision campaign is online at <www.revision.org> and has many helpful resources for various types of groups wanting to get more involved in creation care.

[15]The full statement and signatory list for the Evangelical Climate Initiative can be found at <http://christiansandclimate.org/>.

[16]"A Call to Truth, Prudence, and Protection of the Poor" can be found at <www .cornwallalliance.org/docs/a-call-to-truth-prudence-and-protection-of-the-poor .pdf>.

[17]Read the press release at <www.nae.net/index.cfm?FUSEACTION=editor. page&pageID=413&IDcategory=1>.

[18]Ann Arbor Vineyard Church page, "The Friendship Project" <www. annarborvineyard.org/justice_compassion/green_vineyard.cfm>.

[19]Southern Baptist Environment and Climate Initiative website <www. baptistcreationcare.org/>.

Chapter 5: Spheres of Change

[1]The Creation, I Care website is at <www.creationicare.com/>.

[2]I compiled this rough data for A Rocha outreach purposes by searching through the websites of all the CCCU campuses in February and March of 2008.

[3]See the Association for the Advancement of Sustainability in Higher Education website <www.aashe.org/index.php>.

[4]The College Sustainability Report Card 2008 is found at <www.greenreportcard .org/report-card-2008>.

[5]Two popular lists include *Grist*'s "15 Green Colleges and Universities," available at <http://grist.org/news/maindish/2007/08/10/colleges/>, and *Sierra*'s "Cool Schools," at <www.sierraclub.org/sierra/200711/coolschools/ten.asp>.

[6]More information on the Green Seminary Initiative can be found at <www

.webofcreation.org/GreenSeminary/>.

[7]Edward R. Brown, *Our Father's World: Mobilizing the Church to Care for Creation* (Downers Grove, Ill.: InterVarsity Press, 2008), p. 131.

Chapter 6: Transformation

[1]"Is God Green?" is an excellent introduction to the current creation care scene; segments can be viewed at <www.pbs.org/moyers/moyersonamerica/green/>.

[2]Tri Robinson, *Saving God's Green Earth: Rediscovering the Church's Responsibility to Environmental Stewardship* (Norcross, Ga.: Ampelon Publishing, 2006), and *Small Footprint Big Handprint: How to Live Simply and Love Extravagantly* (Norcross, Ga.: Ampelon Publishing, 2008).

[3]Information on Vineyard Boise's creation care efforts can be found at <www .letstendthegarden.org>.

[4]Personal correspondence by e-mail, December 2007.

[5]Al Hsu shared this and many other helpful personal anecdotes with me as this book was being edited.

[6]EMU is practicing creation care on many fronts; more about their efforts can be found at <http://www.emu.edu/begreen/>.

[7]Data obtained from the Abilene Christian University website <www.acu.edu /campusoffices/adminsvcs/green/Initiatives/index.html>.

[8]Vince Morris was the brain behind this list. Neither of us are aware of an older source for these ideas articulated in this way.

[9]Monterey Bay Aquarium Seafood Watch is available online at <www.mbayaq .org/cr/SeafoodWatch.asp>.

[10]*Greenwashing*, according to the definition provided by Terrachoice, is "the act of misleading consumers regarding the environmental practices of a company or the environmental benefits of a product or service." Found at <www.terrachoice.com /Home/Six%20Sins%20of%20Greenwashing>.

[11]Go to <www.ibiblio.org/lunarbin/worldpop/> to watch the population of the planet grow or shrink second by second.

Chapter 7: Mustard Seed Organizing

[1]Jonathan Isham and Sissel Wage, ed., *Ignition* (Washington, D.C.: Island Press), p. 7.

[2]The full Northland audit can be accessed at <http://creationicare.net/2007/09/ creation-care--.html>.

[3]For more information, go to <www.calvin.edu/admin/provost/ceap/>.

[4]See <www.calvin.edu/admin/provost/scholars/pcw/>.

[5]See <www.grpartners.org/> and <www.ecofoot.msu.edu/miheps/>, respectively.

Chapter 8: Molehills

[1]I first heard it put this way by Nancy Sleeth, and am not aware of an earlier source.
[2]The BBC provides an online guide to what they identify as the world's water hotspots <http://news.bbc.co.uk/2/shared/spl/hi/world/03/world_forum/water/html/ogallala_aquifer.stm>.
[3]Statistics from the EPA Energy Star website <www.energystar.gov/indexcfm?c=cfls.pr_cfls>.

Chapter 9: Sustaining Sustainability

[1]"Report of the World Commission on Environment and Development: Our Common Future," World Commission on Environment and Development, 1987 <www.un-documents.net/wced-ocf.htm>.
[2]More on Gordon College's creation care initiatives can be found at <www.gordon.edu/asf>.
[3]Jeff Greenberg, "An Evolving Creation and Environmental Issues," in *Perspectives on an Evolving Creation* (Grand Rapids: Eerdmans, 2003), pp. 393-413.
[4]For a report of the study and work, see Jeffrey Greenberg, Rudi Seebach, Andrew Luhmann, Deborah Zylstra and Jed Wentz, "Co-operative Sanitation Project, Pellsrus Township, South Africa," *Waterlines* 26, no. 2 (October 2007): pp. 18-21.

Chapter 11: Red, Blue or Green?

[1]I could not think of a way to answer that question in a sound bite without being misunderstood (there are reasons that voting is an anonymous activity). But if I replied that I had voted Republican, then it would be construed that even though I care deeply about the environment, I was willing to put that aside to stick with a party line that consistently favors industry over the environment. If I replied that I voted Democrat, then it would be a sign that the environment was an important enough issue for me to ditch the pro-life Republicans and align with the pro-choice Democrats. In reality, however, I think neither party has a monopoly on Christian values. So I remain an independent.
[2]Newt Gingrich and Terry L. Maple, *A Contract with the Earth* (Baltimore, Md.: Johns Hopkins University Press, 2007).
[3]Jeffrey Sachs, "Common Wealth," *Time*, March 12, 2008 <www.time.com/time/specials/2007/article/0,28804,1720049_1720050_1722057,00.html>.
[4]"Religion and the Presidential Vote: Bush's Gains Broad-Based," The Pew Research Center for the People & the Press, December 6, 2004 <http://people-press.org/commentary/?analysisid=103>.

[5]"Who Would Jesus Vote for?" *Relevant Magazine* <www.relevantmagazine.com/life_article.php?id=7521>.

Chapter 12: We Hug Trees for Jesus
[1]More on the Potter Street Community can be found at <www.thesimpleway.org/index.html>.
[2]The Lausanne Committee on World Evangelization maintains a helpful website with many resources at <www.lausanne.org/>.
[3]Matthew Sleeth, *Serve God, Save the Planet* <www.servegodsavetheplanet.org/?page_id=22>.
[4]Remarks given at the Symposium on Religion, Science, and the Environment, Santa Barbara, California, November 6-8, 1997. From <www.christianecology.org/CarlPope.html>.
[5]Statistic obtained from the Sierra Club Partnerships website at <www.sierraclub.org/partnerships/faith/>.

Epilogue: A Revolution of Hope
[1]The Earth Hour website, which includes information on upcoming events and how to get involved, is found at <www.earthhour.org/>.
[2]Statistic obtained from Bryan Walsh, "Earth Hour '08: Did It Matter?" *Time,* March 27, 2008 <www.time.com/time/health/article/0,8599,1725947,00.html>.
[3]One of St. Francis's most popular writings on creation is "The Canticle of Brother Sun," which can be found online at <www.franciscanfriarstor.com/stfrancis/stf_canticle_of_the_sun.htm>.
[4]Thanks to Paul Steury, education coordinator at Merry Lea Environmental Learning Center, for information on Merry Lea and the many other creation care efforts that Goshen is showing strong leadership in.
[5]This sentence is part of a covenant that the Human Needs and Global Resources program interns at Wheaton College wrote in 2008. Thanks to Nathan Wahl for bringing it to my attention.
[6]Richard J. Foster, *Freedom of Simplicity* (New York: HarperCollins, 1981), p. 164.

LIKEWISE. *Go and do.*

A man comes across an ancient enemy, beaten and left for dead. He lifts the wounded man onto the back of a donkey and takes him to an inn to tend to the man's recovery. Jesus tells this story and instructs those who are listening to "go and do likewise."

Likewise books explore a compassionate, active faith lived out in real time. When we're skeptical about the status quo, Likewise books challenge us to create culture responsibly. When we're confused about who we are and what we're supposed to be doing, Likewise books help us listen for God's voice. When we're discouraged by the troubled world we've inherited, Likewise books encourage us to hold onto hope.

In this life we will face challenges that demand our response. Likewise books face those challenges with us so we can act on faith.

likewisebooks.com